CLERG
A COMPLEX AGE

*Responses to the Guidelines for
the professional conduct of the clergy*

Edited by Jamie Harrison
and Robert Innes

First published in Great Britain in 2016

Society for Promoting Christian Knowledge
36 Causton Street
London SW1P 4ST
www.spck.org.uk

British Library Cataloguing-in-Publication Data
A catalogue record for this book is available from the British Library

ISBN 978–0–281–07492–1
eBook ISBN 978–0–281–07493–8

Typeset by Graphicraft Limited, Hong Kong
First printed in Great Britain by Ashford Colour Press
Subsequently digitally printed in Great Britain

eBook by Graphicraft Limited, Hong Kong

Produced on paper from sustainable forests

Jamie Harrison is a GP specialist adviser to the Care Quality Commission and a former adviser to the Department of Health. He is Research Fellow in Healthcare and Religion at St John's College, Durham University. A long-standing Reader and Member of the Church of England General Synod, he was appointed to the Clergy Discipline Commission in 2014 and elected as Chair of the House of Laity of the General Synod in 2015. He has published widely on issues of vocation, medical careers and the future of the NHS. He received the Baxter Award from the European Health Management Association in 2000 for his book *Clinical Governance in Primary Care*.

Robert Innes is the Church of England's Diocesan Bishop for Europe. Based in Brussels, he oversees clergy and congregations in over 40 different countries and legal jurisdictions. He also represents the Archbishop of Canterbury to the Institutions of the European Union. For many years he taught and ministered in Durham, before moving to Belgium to become Chancellor of the multicultural Pro-Cathedral of Holy Trinity Brussels. His published work ranges from Augustinian theology, through psychological models of selfhood, work and vocation, to the relationship of the Anglican tradition to the Belgian State. He is co-author with Jamie Harrison of *Rebuilding Trust in Healthcare* (2003).

This book is dedicated to

Ruth Etchells (1931–2012)

College principal, scholar, spiritual director,
teacher, faithful friend

Contents

Contents

Part 3
THE FUTURE

Contributors

Kate Bruce is Deputy Warden, Cranmer Hall, Durham.

Paul Butler is Bishop of Durham.

Stephen Cherry is Dean of King's College, Cambridge.

Paula Gooder is Theologian in Residence, The Bible Society.

Jamie Harrison is Fellow in Healthcare and Religion, St John's College, Durham.

Robert Innes is Bishop of Gibraltar in Europe.

Russ Parker is a retired Anglican priest.

John Pritchard is a retired Bishop of Oxford.

Magdalen Smith is Diocesan Director of Ordinands, Chester Diocese.

David Walker is Bishop of Manchester.

Justin Welby is Archbishop of Canterbury.

Foreword

In a complex age with shifting boundaries – sexual, relational, legal and ecclesial – clarity around expectations is immensely helpful. The Guidelines for the professional conduct of the clergy provide a timely and helpful prism through which clergy can discern what it means to be faithful ministers in Christ's Church today. Deacons, priests and bishops are called not only to be custodians of the faith, but also to live exemplary lives of faithfulness and service to others. This is indeed a high calling.

The Guidelines were promulgated by the Convocations of Canterbury and York in July 2015. They were produced by the clergy for the clergy. They carry great moral authority for each member of the clergy, whether paid or self-supporting, in parish or chaplaincy or sector ministry. It is my hope that all our clergy will develop familiarity with the Guidelines and find in them a source of counsel, advice and comfort.

The original Guidelines appeared in 2003. Why? For those coming into ministry in mid-life and from other careers, the absence of professional guidance for the task in hand seemed odd – not what they were used to in medicine, teaching or the law. For others, the Ordinal and Canons proved silent on how to make sense of the internet, safeguarding and the changing nature of society – and its expectations of the clergy. In the Preface to the 2003 Guidelines, the Chairman of the Working Group, Hugh Wilcox, reminded his readers that the 'Guidelines are not a legal code, but a beginning of an ongoing conversation in which ministers and those to whom they minister need to engage.'[1] That ongoing

---

[1] The Convocations of Canterbury and York, *Guidelines for the Professional Conduct of the Clergy*. Church House Publishing, London, 2003, p. ix. The 2015 edition is a major revision of this publication.

conversation has resulted in a revised and updated version of the Guidelines.

This book picks up the conversation. It is not an exegesis of the Guidelines, more of a meditation upon them. After a provocative reflection on what Jesus did and how he related to others (Chapter 1), the book sets the Guidelines firmly in a spiritual context (Chapter 2). It frames them within the charge for each minister to be faithful to his or her calling, a professional man or woman who is trustworthy and deserving of trust (Chapters 3, 11 and 12). It takes particular account of contemporary challenges in regard to safeguarding (Chapter 4). And in intervening chapters (5–10) it sets out a vision for ministry in today's world in dialogue with the Guidelines which I hope will inspire and excite.

Faithful relationships are fundamental to maintaining and improving the life of the Church. It is my fervent desire that increasing trust, particularly that which flows from trustworthy clergy, will transform God's world – a world too often marked by suspicion, scepticism and painful failure.

Justin Welby
Archbishop of Canterbury
Lambeth Palace, London

How this book works

This book is about imagination, explanation and encouragement. It is about hope and faithfulness. It is about trust and being trusted. It is about confident clergy and being confident in clergy. It is about how clergy bring the love of God into all parts of God's world.

In seeking to understand and reflect upon the context and meaning of guidelines for clergy conduct, the book lays out in a series of chapters a vision of how to respond to the complexity and suspicion of the current age. It aims to give clergy renewed joy in the core values and meanings of their calling as ministers of the gospel, while reminding them of the boundaries to that ministry.

So what are we talking about here? Are guidelines for the professional conduct of the clergy (the Guidelines) a rule book for life (a parallel bible?) or a checklist for keeping out of trouble, or both? They are, at least, identifying minimum standards of professional behaviour. But keeping out of trouble might be shorthand for avoiding risk and playing it too safe, when what is needed is a prophetic challenge to the status quo. So at the outset we offer a poem from Stewart Henderson that has a subversive take on priestly ministry, followed by a piece from Paula Gooder (Chapter 1) reminding us that Jesus constantly challenges our expectations and does what we would least expect.

It might seem a bit cheeky that the editors of this book are in one case a member of the laity and in the other a bishop – nevertheless, we hope that the make-up of the team responsible for writing the chapters makes for a nicely balanced group of authors, reflecting the breadth of the Church and a desire to inform and inspire fellow travellers on the Way.

To put one's trust in clergy requires clergy who can be trusted; clergy whose lives are orientated by their faith in Jesus Christ and whose practice is shaped by a perspective on their calling such as that offered by the Guidelines. Yes, such guidelines risk being unrealistic, threatening, undermining. And the shadow cast by 'discipline' can feel long and burdensome. But the Guidelines can also offer a framework and a set of 'rules' to provide comfort, support, guidance and confidence.

The publication *Guidelines for the Professional Conduct of the Clergy 2015*[1] is a collection of documents, which include a foreword from the Archbishops, a preface by the Synodical Secretary of the Convocation of Canterbury, the Guidelines in 14 sections, a theological reflection from Francis Bridger, a note on the ministry of absolution, and one appendix of references plus another relating to safeguarding and relevant documents.

In this book, we print the essential Guidelines as an appendix,[2] and we use relevant, context-setting Ordinal quotes at the head of each chapter. We link the book chapters to Guideline sections, seeking to be creative and without being exact. Where we think two or more guidelines work better together, they go into one chapter. And each chapter author was asked to be imaginative in their writing while remaining faithful to the intention and integrity of the Guidelines themselves.

Given that we did not opt for a one-to-one correspondence between sections in the *Guidelines* publication and chapters in

---

[1] Guidelines for the Professional Conduct of the Clergy published by Church House Publishing. © The Archbishops Council, 2015. Used by permission. <copyright@churchofengland. org.uk>

[2] In this book we use the word 'guideline' for the generic term in relation to guidance, as in 'medical guidelines'. We use 'Guideline' (capital G) to refer to the essential guidance promulgated by the Convocations, as set out in the Appendix to this book. And we use *Guidelines* (italicized) to refer to the volume, *Guidelines for the Professional Conduct of the Clergy 2015, Revised edition*, published by Church House publishing in September 2015 – which contains more than just the Guidelines themselves.

this book, we set out in the table below how the material in the book relates to the relevant Guideline section:

The book in 12 chapters	The 14 related Guidelines
1 Jesus the care-taker	
2 Sustaining the spiritual centre	1: Calling
3 Calling and believing	1: Calling and 8: Faith
4 Staying safe	2: Care and 3: Reconciliation
5 Embodying witness	4: Mission
6 Offering blessing	5: Ministry at times of deepest need
7 Giving leadership	6: Servant leadership
8 Being imaginative	7: Learning and teaching
9 Living faithfully	9: Public ministry and 10: Life and conduct
10 Keeping well	13: Well-being
11 Trusting clergy	12: Trust, 11: Discipline and 14: Care for the carers
12 Faithful servants in a complex age	

So how to use this book? It is a book that can be read front to back or back to front, or just dip in. The central chapters of the book stand on their own, although readers who read from beginning to end will, we hope, see something of a connected flow and argument.

Together the chapters of this book set out a vision for ministry that is concerned with being centred upon Jesus, staying safe, embodying witness, offering blessing, giving leadership, being imaginative, keeping well and living faithfully. Such a ministry builds and rebuilds trust and confidence. It is a simple and clear vision for a complex age. While it is what experienced and competent clergy do routinely, the book contains fresh ideas and perspectives. And so, we hope this book may help our clergy to reflect creatively on their ministries and to calibrate and tune what they do and how they do it in the light of the Guidelines to the greater glory of God and the growth of his kingdom.

Jamie Harrison
Robert Innes

'Priestly duties'[1]

What should a priest be?
All things to all –
male, female and genderless.
What should a priest be?
Reverent and relaxed,
vibrant in youth,
assured through the middle years,
divine sage when aging.

What should a priest be?
Accessible and incorruptible,
abstemious, yet full of celebration,
informed, but not threateningly so,
and far above
the passing soufflé of fashion.

What should a priest be?
An authority on singleness,
Solomon-like on the labyrinth
of human sexuality,
excellent with young marrieds,
old marrieds, were marrieds, never
marrieds, shouldn't have marrieds,
those who live together, those who live
apart, and those who don't live anywhere,
respectfully mindful of senior
citizens and war veterans,
familiar with the ravages of arthritis,
osteoporosis, post-natal depression,
anorexia, whooping-cough and nits.

[1] Henderson, S., 'Priestly duties' (written for Eric Delve, 23.5.96), published in *Limited Edition*. Plover Books, London, 1997, p. 21; reproduced with permission.

What should a priest be?
All-round family person,
counsellor, but not officially because
of the recent changes in legislation,
teacher, expositor, confessor,
entertainer, juggler,
good with children, and
possibly sea-lions,
empathetic towards pressure-groups.

What should a priest be?
On nodding terms with
Freud, Jung, St John of the Cross,
The Scott Report, The Rave Culture,
The Internet, The Lottery, BSE and
Anthea Turner,
pre-modern, fairly modern,
post-modern, and, ideally,
secondary-modern –
if called to the inner city.

What should a priest be?
Charismatic, if needs must,
but quietly so,
evangelical, and thoroughly,
meditative, mystical, but not
New Age.
Liberal, and so open to other voices,
traditionalist, reformer and
revolutionary
and hopefully, not on medication
unless for an old sporting injury.

Note to congregations

If your priest actually fulfils all of the above, and
then enters the pulpit one Sunday morning wearing

nothing but a shower-cap, a fez, and declares 'I'm the
King and Queen of Venus, and we shall now sing the
next hymn, in Latvian, take your partners please'–
Let it pass.
Like you and I,
they too sew the thin thread of humanity.
Remember Jesus in the Garden –
beside himself?

So, what does a priest do?
Mostly stays awake
at Deanery synods.
Tries not to annoy the Bishop
too much,
visits hospices, administers comfort,
conducts weddings, christenings –
not necessarily in that order,
takes funerals,
consecrates the elderly to the grave,
buries children and babies,
feels completely helpless beside
the swaying family of a suicide.

What does a priest do?
Tries to colour in God,
uses words to explain miracles,
which is like teaching
a millipede to sing, but
even more difficult.
What does a priest do?
Answers the phone
when sometimes they'd rather not,
occasionally errs and strays
into tabloid titillation,
prays for Her Majesty's Government.

'Priestly duties'

What does a priest do?
Tends the flock through time,
oil and incense,
would secretly like each PCC
to commence
with a mud-pie making contest,
sometimes falls asleep when praying,
yearns, like us, for
heart-rushing deliverance.

What does a priest do?
Has rows with their family,
wants to inhale Heaven,
stares at bluebells,
attempts to convey the mad love of God,
would like to ice-skate with crocodiles,
and hear the roses when they pray.

How should a priest live?

How should we live?

As priests –
transformed by The Priest
that death prised open
so that he could be our priest –
martyred, diaphanous and
matchless priest.

What should a priest be?

What should a priest do?

How should a priest live?

How should we live . . . ?

Part 1
SETTING THE SCENE

1

Jesus the care-taker

PAULA GOODER

> Among all God's actions there is none which is not entirely
> a matter of mercy, love and compassion: this constitutes the
> beginning and end of His dealing with us.
>
> (St Isaac of Syria)

What would Jesus do? It is a question to strike fear into the hearts
of most New Testament scholars. Don't get me wrong, it is an
important question – a vital question even. The problem is how
to answer it with any level of certainty or accuracy. It is a simple
question, suggesting that the most appropriate response would be
to provide an equally simple answer. The problem is that the Jesus
we meet in the pages of the Gospels rather defies simple answers.

Part of the challenge is our images of Jesus. There are almost
as many images of Jesus as there are people picturing him: from
'gentle Jesus, meek and mild' to Jesus the activist intent on over-
turning the secular or religious mores of his day; from a wise
teacher to a doer of good deeds; from a friend of the poor and
the outcast to a powerfully influential man who has friends among
the rich and the powerful; from a political revolutionary to the
fulfilment of all Israel's hopes and dreams.

The list gets longer with every new person who attempts to
capture an answer to the disciples' question in Mark 4.41, 'Who
then is this?' As the list grows it is worth reminding ourselves of
the words of George Tyrrell who likened the quest for the Historical
Jesus to scholars seeing their own reflection in the bottom of a

3

deep well.[1] Try as we might, it is all too easy to make Jesus in our own image. The reality of Jesus was somewhat different. As you read through the Gospels it becomes very clear that no one image of Jesus can hope to capture the real Jesus.

This real Jesus defies description. He was gentle but also fiercely passionate; he was a wise teacher but also did much good; he was a friend of the poor and outcast but also of the rich and the powerful; the out-workings of his politics were revolutionary but he was also the fulfilment of all Israel's hopes. Jesus was a both/and rather than an either/or person. The only thing we can say with any level of certainty about him is that he cannot be tied down.

Tempting as it might be, therefore, to try and imagine how Jesus would have lived out the Guidelines for the professional conduct of the clergy, any wise New Testament scholar avoids getting mired too deeply in such a knotty question. The best answer to the question, 'What would Jesus do?' is mostly likely to be, 'The last thing you expect'. Jesus broke the mould of expectation time and time again and was most often to be found in the last place people thought to look (as he was at the age of 12 when his parents were looking for him, Luke 2.41–50), with the people you might least expect him to mix with, doing something you never imagined to be possible.

We might struggle to be confident about what Jesus *would* do in any given situation but we do know what he *did* do, in all its breadth and depth. This led me to wonder therefore whether it might be possible to draw guidelines for conduct from the Gospels themselves, from what Jesus did do and how he related to others. What follows are just a few possible guidelines that we might want to draw from Jesus' life and example. There are many more, and as you read you might like to ponder which ones you would add to the list.

---

[1] Tyrrell, G., *Christianity at the Crossroads*. Longmans, Green & Co., London, 1909, p. 44.

Engage with the person, not the stereotype

If there is a strand that runs all the way through Jesus' ministry it is that he engaged with people as they really were, rather than as you might imagine them to be. This is one of the factors that leads to Jesus acting unexpectedly time and time again. It is a part of human nature to categorize people. It helps us process vast amounts of information quickly and efficiently and to know where we stand in the world. The problem is that people aren't library books – and it must be said that even books are quite hard to categorize! I have lost count of the number of times people have said to me, '. . . but what are you?' Depending on the context of the question, they are asking for an easy label to apply to me which will then allow them to surmise what I think about a large range of topics.

Throughout the pages of the Gospels we see people who are similarly labelled: tax collectors, sinners, Gentiles, 'the ill'. Outsiders, all of them, their label ensured that those who had never met them knew to stay away and not to engage with them at all. The most fascinating example of this is the label 'sinner', which often appears in an epithet with 'tax collector'. Where tax collector is a job description it is hard to imagine what job one did to fulfil the job description of 'sinner'. The consensus is that they were people who had contravened the law on more than one occasion and so were deemed unworthy for inclusion among the society of the righteous.

Jesus is often to be found in their company, talking to them, eating with them and simply seeing them for who they really were. This is a characteristic that comes through strongly in Jesus' encounter with the Samaritan woman in John 4. Despite popular opinion, we don't actually know whether she was a 'sinner' deserving of the job title or not. She had had five husbands and now lived with someone to whom she was not married (4.18). We do not know whether she had been divorced five times or whether her husbands had died (or a combination of the two). In any case women could not divorce their husbands: only men could divorce women, not the other way around. If she *was* divorced it could have been for adultery or for something much more trivial than that (Rabbi Hillel is renowned for allowing divorce if a wife burns a meal). In addition the law forbade someone to be married more than five times, so she had no option but not to be married to the sixth person. She may or may not have been a sinner but she *was* vulnerable. Only women who were isolated in society would go to a well alone in the heat of the day. In the midst of her misery and loneliness, she met Jesus and felt truly 'seen' by him ('Come and see a man who told me everything I have ever done!' John 4.29).

It is important, however, not to swing the pendulum too far. People love to say that Jesus was a friend of the poor and the outcast. They are right, he was. This does not, by extension, mean that he avoided the rich and powerful. He treated them no better and no worse than the poor and outcast. Again he saw them for who they were and listened to what they needed. Throughout the Gospels we can observe Jesus' encounter with a number of rich people: for example, Nicodemus (one of the Sanhedrin); Joseph of Arimathea (in whose tomb Jesus was buried); Simon the Pharisee (with whom Jesus dined, Luke 7.36). Most intriguing of all is the giveaway reference in John's Gospel to one of the disciples (often assumed to be the beloved disciple) being known to the high priest (John 18.15), thereby suggesting that Jesus might have had earlier encounters with these leaders of Jewish society.

The best example of all, however, is the string of stories in Mark's Gospel (chapters 4–8) in which Jesus encountered and transformed a number of outsiders: the Gerasene demoniac (a Gentile and someone possessed by a demon), the woman with a haemorrhage (someone rendered permanently unclean by her bleeding), the Syrophoenician woman (a Gentile woman), a man who could not hear or speak and then a man who was blind. All were outcasts, some doubly so. In the middle of this string of outsiders, however, we read of Jesus' encounter with Jairus. Jairus was the leader of the Synagogue, an establishment figure who was no doubt wealthy and powerful. Jesus responded to him just as he did to all the others. Again, he saw him for who he was in the midst of his need and responded to him like that.

One of the greatest challenges for pastoral care is cultivating the ability to see people as they are. Not to jump to conclusions about them because of any preconceived conceptions we might have, but to see *them*, to love *them* as they are and for who they are.

Don't hide your vulnerability

We have already mentioned Jesus' encounter with the Samaritan woman but it is worth returning to the narrative again for one more insight about Jesus' encounter with people during his ministry. The striking feature of Jesus' conversation with the Samaritan woman is that it took place while Jesus was himself at a low ebb. John tells us that Jesus was 'tired out by his journey' (4.6): he was exhausted and so had sat down for a rest. In need of water, he reached out for help to the Samaritan woman – it was this action of reaching out that enabled the conversation to happen in the first place. We can't know for sure but it is probable that the woman felt more able to be open with Jesus because she saw him in need.

There is, of course, a fine line between being prepared to be vulnerable with others and splurging your own need onto someone else. The key seems to be to keep it in balance. The presentation of too smooth and assured an exterior means people will not feel able to share their own vulnerability; too great an openness in the wrong context can make that encounter more about you than the other person. It is intriguing to notice that there are a few occasions in the Gospels (particularly here and in John 11.35) where we see Jesus' true self, his vulnerability, weariness and grief, but on the whole we know very little about Jesus' thoughts on the world of his day. His focus was outwards onto other people and their need. He was prepared to be vulnerable when necessary but didn't dwell on it.

Take care of yourself but be guided by compassion

This brings us to a similar pattern of behaviour that we can observe all the way through the Gospels: Jesus was attuned to his own well-being and ministered out of this. When he was tired, he rested. When he needed to pray, he withdrew. When he became aware of hostility, he would often leave. Jesus took care of himself and his needs, giving himself time and space for recuperation and refreshment.

At the same time he was prepared for that space to be encroached upon when people were in need. In John 6.1–2 Jesus went up the mountain with his disciples, one presumes to have some time alone with them, but then fed the five thousand when a large crowd followed him. In Matthew 14.13 Jesus withdrew in a boat to a deserted place, but when he saw the crowd who had followed him he had compassion upon them and healed them. Again the key seems to be balance: sufficient time alone for refreshment but a willingness to break that when necessary.

One of the words that returns time and time again through-out the Gospels is the word 'compassion'. The Greek is the splendid-sounding *splangchnizomai* which means literally to have a movement in the bowels. It describes a feeling of compassion so strong that you feel it physically. One of the striking features of this word is that it is a verb used exclusively to describe Jesus and his relationship with those he met (see Matthew 9.36; 4.23–24; 20.34), with one exception – it is also the verb used to describe the emotion of the good Samaritan when he saw the man who had been attacked by thieves. In other words it is a 'Jesus' word used to describe what Jesus felt when he encountered those in need.

It is a word that should be the byword for all pastoral ministry. If we have compassion for others but also, and crucially, for ourselves then we will be beginning to follow something of the pattern of Jesus' life and conduct.

Avoid getting sucked into live issues that can't be resolved

This guideline may appear to be out of kilter with the others mentioned so far but is something that is particularly noticeable in Jesus' ministry. Jesus rarely answered questions directly. His most common response to a question was another question. This is especially true when the question appears designed to trip him up or to ask him to declare his view on a knotty modern issue. Take, for example, the lawyer in Luke 10.25 who asked Jesus what he had to do to inherit eternal life. In Jesus' day this would have been a profoundly loaded question. The question was really asking Jesus whether he aligned himself with the Pharisees and the Essenes, who did believe in life after death, or with the Sadducees (that is, the high priests and others) who did not.

Jesus did not answer the lawyer's question. Instead he asked a question back ('What is written in the law? What do you read there?' Luke 10.26). The lawyer, not prepared to let Jesus off the hook, asked his own question back to Jesus ('And who is my neighbour?' 10.29), at which point Jesus took a different tack and told a story – the story of the good Samaritan. What is interesting about the encounter is that Jesus appeared to keep an eye, again, on the needs of the lawyer. He was, as always, compassionate and sought out different methods of conversation that might allow the lawyer to be transformed and to understand who Jesus really was. Sadly we don't know what happened to him but the story still resonates. If Jesus had allowed himself to be sucked into controversial theological debate, then the potential for transforming the lawyer would have been diminished.

Be prepared to be corrected

My fifth guideline is probably my most controversial, since it all depends on how you read Jesus' discussion with the Syrophoenician

9

woman in Mark 7.25–30 and Matthew 15.21–28. My own view is that this unnamed woman patiently, gently but inexorably showed Jesus that his Israel-only focus was wrong, and that she too deserved to benefit from the good news of the kingdom. If I am right, then this story shows that Jesus was prepared to be corrected, to see things through a new lens and to be changed by his encounters with others.

This is not always easy to do. The ability to change graciously and generously is one that we all wrestle with – but it is vital to good, healthy relationships.

Concluding reflections

The list of guidelines drawn from the Gospels could go on and on, but what I have tried to do is to pick those ones that demonstrate why it is so difficult to answer the question 'What would Jesus do?' It is difficult because Jesus was, as the title of this piece intimates, the ultimate 'care-taker'. His ministry was characterized by compassion – compassion for those he met and compassion for himself. He took care to listen to people and to see them for who they were. He was prepared to reveal, though not to dwell on, his vulnerabilities. He took good care of himself but was prepared to break his time of refreshment when the moment required. He avoided getting sucked into arguments to which there were no answers, looking instead for opportunities to help the person asking to be transformed, and he was prepared, if necessary, to have his vision widened, broadened and deepened.

What would Jesus do? He would 'take care': profound, gut-wrenching, compassionate care – and he calls us to do the same.

References

Tyrrell, G., *Christianity at the Crossroads*. Longmans, Green and Co., London, 1909.

2

Sustaining the spiritual centre

JOHN PRITCHARD

Will you be diligent in prayer, in reading Holy Scripture?
(The Ordinal)

You cannot bear the weight of this calling in your own strength,
but only by the grace and power of God. Pray therefore that
your heart may daily be enlarged and your understanding of
the Scriptures enlightened. Pray earnestly for the gift of the
Holy Spirit. (The Ordinal)

I often ask Christian groups what season of the year they feel
themselves to be in spiritually. Is it spring, a time when so much
is in bud, full of rich possibility and new experiences of God's
presence? Or is it high summer when life is in full colour, prayer
is a joy and God is glimpsed at every turn? Or perhaps autumn
is a better description; there is ripeness and maturity, a time of
harvest, but also a time when the more exotic fruits have gone
and the occasional frost speaks of changes to come. Or maybe it
is winter, a time of cold days and long nights, of dark perplexity
and hard silence, when we can only trust that something significant
is going on below ground.

Thinking about our spiritual well-being as a month in the cycle
of the seasons can be a helpful, imaginative way of reflecting on
the most important dimension of a priest's experience, the health
of his or her spiritual life.

Even calling it a 'spiritual life' runs many dangers. What is a
spiritual life as opposed to the rest of life? Isn't life a unity? It's

not as if there are parts of life that God hasn't found yet. God can't ever be somewhere else, doing something else, only making the occasional guest appearance to do God-like things when invited. 'The earth is the Lord's and all that is in it' (Psalm 24.1) and 'all that is in it' presumably means the time I spend walking the dog, shopping in the supermarket, watching cricket on the television and arguing with the traffic warden. God can never be absent from a world of God's making; we're the only ones who can be absent.

Nevertheless, for shorthand, let's use the slippery word 'spirituality' and explore a number of angles on the fundamental task of the priest that is to stay in touch with the living God. From that, all else flows.

A spirituality of desire

Above all else, a priest has to desire God. 'As a deer longs for flowing streams, so my soul longs for you, O God. My soul thirsts for God, for the living God. When shall I come and behold the face of God?' (Psalm 42.1–2). We live in the attentive gaze of God and perhaps our life's task is to return that gaze with joy and confidence. This needs to be the case even if that desire almost feels like nostalgia because the vivid immediacy of God has waned and the divine trail has gone cold. In the well-known words of Archbishop Michael Ramsey, 'If in sincerity you cannot say that you want God, you can perhaps tell him that you want to want him, and if you cannot say even that, perhaps you can say that you want to want to want him.'[1]

It may be hard to remain white hot in our desire for God year after year but we might be at least challenged by this tale from the Desert Fathers.

> Abbot Lot came to Abbot Joseph and said: 'Father, according as I am able, I keep my little rule, and my little fast, my

---

[1] Ramsey, M., *The Christian Priest Today*. SPCK, London, 1972, reissued 2009, p. 14.

prayer, meditation and contemplative silence; and according as I am able I strive to cleanse my heart of thoughts: now what more should I do?' The elder rose up in reply and stretched out his hands to heaven, and his fingers became like ten lamps of fire. And he said: 'Why not be totally changed into fire?'[2]

How a priest makes the desire for God a priority is a matter of individual detailed decisions. There's no point in generalizing. At this stage it's sufficient to note that it's the direction of gaze that matters supremely, the desire for God, longing to be taken into the life and heart of God.

A spirituality of attentiveness

At the heart of ministry is attentiveness: attentiveness to God and attentiveness to people. In a restless, distracted culture, giving other people undivided attention is a gift as precious as it's rare. That gift flows, I believe, from learning to attend to God with similar focus. The point about prayer is not to think of it just as a specialized activity called 'prayer' but to think of it as being entranced by the reality of God. The overflow of that attentiveness is that priests begin to see all of life in the light of God, and increasingly to be able to focus on, and stay with, the person before them.

It goes even further: as we develop attentiveness we might sense a deeper reverence for life in all its parts, not just its human dimension. One exercise that helps to develop that reverence is to spend 20 minutes looking closely at a square yard of ground (even better at water's edge) and to notice the extraordinary variety, delicacy, richness, colour, texture, density, movement and shape of what lies before us. Instead of walking carelessly over the earth, we might learn to be reverent, careful and respectful both of

---

[2] Merton, T., *The Wisdom of the Desert. Sayings from the Desert Fathers of the Fourth Century.* New Directions, New York, 1960, p. 50.

creation and the Creator. Philip Toynbee said, 'The central command of religion isn't "do this" or "don't do that" but simply "look".'[3]

It is not hard to see that this attentiveness to whatever lies before us spills over into the social and political spheres as well. Really to notice what's going on in the communities we serve, and being aware of the dangers and limitations of living in a church bubble, is the beginning of a deeper social engagement as we build the kingdom brick by brick and share God's goal of healing creation.

A rhythmic spirituality

One of the discoveries that those coming fresh to the Anglican Church seem to value most is the gift of rhythm and shape in prayer and worship, patterns that hold us in good times and bad. On a retreat a simple rhythm of morning and evening prayer, midday Eucharist and compline at night creates a holding pattern in which the day rests comfortably. Anglican priests are expected to say Morning and Evening Prayer as part of the responsibilities laid on them by canon law. This isn't meant to be a punitive regime but rather a liberating framework. Not all clergy keep to that precise requirement but without some Godly pattern of prayer we are much the poorer, and much more vulnerable to running out of spiritual steam. Those priests who use a clear framework find not so much that they are sustaining the pattern of prayer as that the pattern of prayer is sustaining them. Woody Allen said that 80 per cent of life is just showing up, and this is particularly true of daily prayer. Just being there is almost enough. The Desert Fathers said, 'Go to your cell, and your cell will teach you everything.'

A spirituality with depth

If we remain content to play in the shallows of Christian spirituality we short-change ourselves, God and the people we serve.

---

[3] Toynbee, P., *Part of a Journey*. Collins, London, 1981, entry for 15 February 1978.

God is not shallow. We usually enter the waters of faith believing that this wonderful experience is happening in an Olympic-sized swimming pool; only later do we find we're on the edge of a limitless ocean. God is so much bigger than we ever imagined. Or if not, we haven't yet encountered the true scale and intensity of divine grace. If we aren't out of our depth and beyond our own safety limits then we're still playing children's games on the beach, and while that may be fun for a while it's unlikely to satisfy us in the longer term. Moreover, it won't satisfy our more thoughtful and enquiring lay people who are keen to grow and discover more of the riches of Christ. One alarming large-scale piece of research in the United States found that 63 per cent of the most committed members were considering leaving their churches because they simply weren't being fed. They wanted more, and the church leaders weren't offering it.

My father once warned me of the tragedy of a 100 per cent surrender to a 10 per cent idea of Jesus Christ. The same might be said of a 100 per cent commitment to a 10 per cent understanding of the riches and depth of the Christian spiritual tradition. There's always more.

A spirituality with breadth

When I think back to the spiritual diet I had at ordination I remain deeply grateful for what I had been given but even more grateful for what I've found since. The Bible, the Eucharist and a simple (mainly intercessory) style of prayer have been supplemented by elements of Franciscan, Celtic, Benedictine and Ignatian spiritualities, retreats in various delectable settings, regular visits to Taizé, pilgrimages to many holy places and conversations with many holy people, individually guided retreats, icons, Iona, cathedrals, the power of silence and contemplative prayer, praise music and choral evensong, and much more. I've found so many different ways to feed on Scripture and a plethora of ways to stimulate the imagination in prayer. I remain a serial beginner in prayer, no expert, but if I'd stayed in the shallow end I might have perished of boredom.

It's important for priests to be self-aware enough to be humble, and graceful enough to be generous, in guiding others on their own completely unique spiritual journeys. The self-awareness comes in not riding our own spiritual hobby-horses to the point of exhaustion. It is enhanced by engaging the wisdom of a spiritual director, for as the Guidelines remind us in section 14.6, 'All the clergy should . . . be encouraged to have a spiritual director, soul friend or confessor to support their spiritual life and help to develop their growth in self-understanding.' Our way of praying is only *one* way, not *the only* way. It might have helped us to come singing and dancing into the kingdom but it might equally scare others to death or bore them to sleep. The graceful generosity comes in knowing other wells of spiritual water and being able to commend them, even if they don't quench much of our own thirst. Clergy are there to serve, not dictate; to signpost, not point to themselves.

A *worldly spirituality*

That sounds dangerous! What I mean is that priests need to feel at home both in the world of church and the world where 'church' doesn't even register, if we are to be interpreters of the one to the other. Theologically, I don't want to have to choose between reading the Bible and smelling the wind off the sea or being enchanted by a new film or an old painting. Whoever persuaded me that God preferred four frescoed walls and a fancy roof to the everyday struggles of men and women seeking to live fully and freely in a world of politics and power? God is at home everywhere in God's world.

So priests need to be at home in both worlds, as Jesus was. Jesus did the majority of his teaching outside designated sacred spaces.

The tools he used weren't liturgy and systematic theology but ears of wheat, old wineskins, rebellious sons, last-minute labourers and foolish entrepreneurs. We, similarly, need to be at home in the world of church and the world where 'church' is an esoteric puzzle – or we won't understand our neighbour. We need to be at home in the world of Sunday and of Monday, or our faith will be disconnected from most of life. We need to be at home in the world of certainty and of doubt, or we won't understand our culture. We need to be at home in the world of safe answers and of disturbing questions, or we won't be equipped to be witnesses.

If we inhabit the borderlands of these different worlds we'll meet other explorers, interpreters, artists, poets, researchers, lovers, philosophers and prophets. This is where the exciting conversations go on, when we politely excuse ourselves from discussing the church drains or the latest liturgical revision and go out to meet the rest of the world for which Christ lived, died and rose again. Be worldly, but be rooted in Christ.

A spirituality of failure

This might sound extreme, but if we follow a man who died publically and painfully on a cross as a result of a shoddy collaboration of powerful men, we shouldn't be surprised at our own failures as we seek to announce the kingdom to a largely deaf world. The point about having a specific spirituality of failure is that if we haven't worked through the dynamics of struggle and failure we might crash and burn at some point because we have insufficient resources to cope with these situations.

Congregations drift down in numbers, conflicts rip a church apart, clergy get too close to parishioners, cherished schemes wither away, a mission attracts nobody new, money is running out. We have our PR justifications of course; we convince some in the church; we even convince ourselves on a good day with a following wind.

But in the middle of the night we know the truth: humanly we're on the rocks. I don't know any priest with a number of years of ministry behind him or her, even in apparently 'successful' churches, who hasn't been through a dark night.

Living at a time when growth and success are cultural obsessions makes following a crucified prophet a difficult proposition. Priests flourish best when they've accepted that their call is to faithfulness rather than success, and that God is the missioner anyway; we just have to get into God's slipstream and enjoy the ride. The motif of death and resurrection isn't simply a theoretical concept but a lived reality carved into the nature of human experience. Much may have to die in our inherited ways of church organization and practice, but that's part of the rhythm of discipleship. 'Don't be afraid' was the phrase most often on the lips of Jesus. The last word is always with resurrection. Always.

A spirituality of joy

Why would anyone be attracted to a gospel offered by a grumpy priest? Faith is usually passed on as a kind of divine infection and the carrier of that infection is often a joyful priest. Not that we can make ourselves joyful. I know of one house where the owners, for a reason I never fully understood, tied lemons on to a tree in their front garden. Not surprisingly, people weren't fooled. We know when we meet the genuine fruit of a Christ-centred life. Our goal, then, is not so much to be joyful but to be so open to the life of Christ that the fruit simply drips from the tree.

There are, however, ways of encouraging joy. When we look at life 'gold side up', always trying to see the original blessing, then joy flows more naturally into and through our lives. Thankfulness seems to be another key; once we take thankfulness seriously we find there's more and more for which to be thankful. Another contribution comes from the discipline of laughter; sometimes we have to give ourselves permission to laugh more, to watch more comedy, to lighten up. Remember that it takes more muscles to frown than to laugh.

The fruit of the Spirit is love, joy and peace (Galatians 5.22).

A spirituality of hope

Christianity in the West is in a time of uncertainty – some would say crisis. It's undoubtedly the case that there are tectonic shifts going on in our culture that are changing the geology of faith and causing some to take cover in their equivalent of Eeyore's Gloomy Place. One of the gifts that the Church needs from its clergy is that of hope, not of the 'whistling in the dark' variety but hope drawn from trust in a God who knows the way out of a grave, or indeed a God the scale of whose ambition isn't a few more people coming to church but the wholesale renewal of creation.

Archbishop Desmond Tutu once encouraged an audience by saying, 'I've read to the end of the book. We win!' This should translate not into triumphalism but into a quiet confidence that this is God's world and God's purposes are ultimately guaranteed. In the meantime, as Christian activist Jim Wallis wrote, 'Hope is believing in spite of the evidence, and then watching the evidence change.'[4] The priest cultivates rootedness in the past, passion for the present and confidence in God's future. And it's the future which draws us, as iron to the magnet of God's love. That promise is one to claim every new day and for all eternity.

So what?

One of the core tasks of priests today is to make sure that the scent of God doesn't disappear from our culture. We live at a bewildering time where it seems that we scoop up experiences

---

[4] Wallis, J., in Loeb, P. J., *The Impossible will Take a Little While*. Basic Books, New York, 2004, p. 203.

without considering their meaning, and deal with anxiety by buying something new. Speed is seen as a virtue and slow is seen as sin; society constantly urges us to hurry up. In such a context the priest-like task is to invite people to take a slower speed, a human speed, the speed at which God walks. At this speed we have time to reflect on the meaning of our experiences, the value of our purchases, the purpose of living at speed. The air may be full of exotic smells but none compares with the original perfume of paradise, and that can only fill our lives when we savour the sights, scents and sounds of the journey we're on.

If priests are going to invite people into this world of the senses then we have to experience them ourselves. We have to walk at God's speed, the speed of love. Our first priority is to sustain the sacred centre and to find there a spring of living water bubbling up to eternal life.

References

Loeb, P. J., *The Impossible will Take a Little While.* Basic Books, New York, 2004.

Merton, T., *The Wisdom of the Desert. Sayings from the Desert Fathers of the Fourth Century.* New Directions, New York, 1960.

Ramsey, M., *The Christian Priest Today.* SPCK, London, 1972, reissued 2009.

Toynbee, P., *Part of a Journey.* Collins, London, 1981.

3

Calling and believing

ROBERT INNES

Priests are to set the example of the Good Shepherd always
before them as the pattern of their calling.   (The Ordinal)

No doubt the same may be said of all professions. They are
all conspiracies against the laity.   (George Bernard Shaw)

Leadership in challenging times

Old Testament leaders have 'form' when it comes to being shepherds. Abraham kept sheep in the ancient city of Ur. Moses received
his decisive call from God when looking after his father-in-law's
flocks, and David was a shepherd boy long before he was selected
to be king over Israel. The Old Testament prophets looked forward
to a leader who would be the good and true shepherd of their
people. In the words of Isaiah, immortalised by the composer
Handel, 'He shall feed his flock like a shepherd, and he shall
gently lead those that are with young.'

So when Jesus says 'I am the good shepherd' he fulfils a thousand
years of hope and expectation. As the shepherd who lays down
his life for the sheep, Jesus provides the model of self-sacrificing
pastoral leadership. It is to this model that those who have the
vocation to be priests and pastors are invited to aspire at their
ordination.

Yet the model, of shepherd and sheep, is not without its problems for modern people. It seems demeaning to describe the

adults who populate our churches as sheep, not least as today we value human autonomy so highly. And the guidelines for today's schools of counselling do not encourage the sort of 'directiveness' that seems to be an inherent part of the shepherd's role. But, in many respects, human beings are as sheep-like as ever. We follow the crowds and follow the fashions. We still err and stray from the ways of the Lord like lost sheep. And we long as much as we ever did for good and wise leadership – not just in the Church but in public life more generally.

Against the high and beautiful aspirations of the Ordinal, it is rather shocking, but nonetheless realistic, to set the suspicion of professional elites enunciated by Shaw in his play *The Doctor's Dilemma*. Shaw's criticism, noted above, has become a well-known quotation. It was the doctors that he had foremost in his sights. But other professions – the law, the clergy – were not spared. For Shaw, professions, with their own carefully tended body of expertise, gained money, power or prestige from those in whose interests they claimed to be working and so were inherently suspect.[1]

A century after Shaw, this critique has intensified. It is now commonplace to talk about a 'crisis of trust', whether in regard to politicians, financiers, doctors or clergy.[2] In her 2002 Reith Lectures, the moral philosopher Onora O'Neill explored the phenomenon, wondering whether we really do trust less than we used to, or whether it is just that we say we are less trusting. Perhaps, she suggests, it would be more accurate to talk of a climate of suspicion rather than actual mistrust (see Chapter 11).[3] But in the 13 years since O'Neill's lectures, the climate has, if anything, worsened: MPs' expenses, the war in Iraq and, most especially, allegations and findings of child abuse perpetrated by people in high places,

---

[1] Shaw, G. B., *The Doctor's Dilemma*. Penguin, New York, 1946.
[2] For example, in relation to the medical profession, see Harrison, J., Innes, R. and van Zwanenberg, T. (eds), *Rebuilding Trust in Healthcare*. Radcliffe Medical Press, Oxford, 2003.
[3] O'Neill, O., *A Question of Trust*. Cambridge University Press, Cambridge, 2002.

have further undermined public trust in national institutions and their representatives.

Yet we long for good leaders and 'shepherdly' care. When our personal lives hit rough times we search out those who will be genuinely 'for us' in giving wise, honest and caring counsel. At a national level, the 'Nolan principles' still provide inspiring ideals for those in public life to which we would dearly hope our MPs, civil servants and health trust board members will adhere.[4] And if the public seeks high ethical standards from secular leaders, then standards of at least as high a level will be expected from those called to leadership in the Church.

Those who respond to a call to ordained ministry are entering this gap between public disenchantment with leaders on the one hand and powerful longings for leaders in whom we can put our trust on the other.

A calling to ordained ministry

I suppose like many others, I began to open my ears and heart to the possibility of a calling to ordained ministry because I wanted to make a difference. In my late twenties I found the work I was doing stimulating, my colleagues of high calibre and the financial rewards surprisingly good. But I was hard-pushed to explain just whose lives were made better through the business strategy we had developed, say, for corporation X or the new administrative systems we had implemented for bank Y.

My wife Helen and I talked things over with a mature couple at our local church. 'You should think about being ordained,' they said. The idea had never previously crossed my mind. No one in my family was ordained. I enjoyed the high adrenalin environment of the business world. And while I sincerely wanted to serve God,

---

[4] The Committee on Standards in Public Life, chaired by Lord Nolan, formulated in 1995 the following principles in relation to public appointments: selflessness, integrity, objectivity, accountability, openness, honesty and leadership.

the Church of England did not figure on my list of 'institutions I have always wanted to work for'.

But the idea refused to go away. An encouraging conversation with my vicar was followed by a series of more demanding conversations with the Director of Ordinands. Like Moses, I could think of some strong reasons why the Lord should choose someone else. My parents were horrified and did everything possible to talk me out of the idea. Helen bravely stood with me, albeit apprehensive that the young man she had married was toying with a very different form of life, which would have major implications for her. Eventually, after three years of soul searching and the deliberations of a selection committee I was recommended for ordination. When I told my work colleagues the news they were – to my great surprise – hugely supportive. There was real delight that one of their number had found something to which he could give his life in a committed and purposeful way. As one of my colleagues said, 'I wish I had something that I believed in to the same degree.'

The sense of being able to give one's life to an occupation in which one truly believes is, indeed, a wonderful gift. For so many, work, where you are lucky enough to have it, is arduous or boring, or both. The TV series *The Rise and Fall of Reginald Perrin* captured well the sense of frustration felt by the middle-aged executive condemned to spending his life commuting to a job that involves selling a product he doesn't believe in. Those of us who are ordained are fortunate to be engaged directly in the work of bringing about God's purposes on earth. Can there be a higher calling? That is something to remember and to treasure.

Growing in faith

The sporty, white, company VW Golf GTi car had to be returned to the leasing company, and I bought a second-hand, family-friendly, red VW Jetta instead. One memorable September morning, Helen, our new baby Ruth and I drove up the A1 from our former home in Beckenham to our new home in Durham. Capital Radio, with its inevitably London-centric view of the UK, provided accompaniment for the first part of the journey with a feature on 'is there intelligent life north of Watford?' Dvorak's Ninth Symphony, intended by Capital to evoke northern grimness through its associations with the well-known Hovis advert, in fact summoned us to a new world and a new home in a two-up two-down mining cottage on the Ushaw Moor road out of Durham.

While there were obvious financial sacrifices in starting theological college, in every other respect I experienced the change as pure gain. I had the immense privilege of being liberated to study for three years. Long hours working in business were replaced by time for personal development and education. And, rather unexpectedly, I fell in love with theology! Having come from a technical and engineering background, I had the sensation of vistas of knowledge opening up before me. I stood on the brink of a whole new world of learning about how God had revealed himself, God's dealings through history with humanity, and the nature and purpose of human life at its deepest level.

There were well-meaning church friends who warned me about the dangers of studying theology. Would my faith not be compromised or corrupted? In a sense, their concerns were justified. For in truth, proper theological learning does have a *negative* component. The spiritual growth which occurs through theological study requires a stripping away of false ideas about God. Just as in the teaching of science, more primitive models have to be 'unlearned' in order for more adequate models to take their place. Indeed, it could be said that one of the major tasks of theological education is the purging of idolatry. That is a potentially painful and risky process.

The poet-theologian Samuel Coleridge expressed well the truth-seeking which is at the heart of the educational-theological project in the following aphorism:

He who begins by loving Christianity better than truth
Will proceed by loving his own sect or church better
    than Christianity,
And end in loving himself best of all.[5]

Coleridge warns that those who fail to attend to the truth risk
entering a spiral that becomes narrower and narrower until it
ends in advocating a religion that is merely a cloak for one's own
self-love. My own later experience as a theological college teacher
was that those who inhabited enclosed systems which they would
not allow to be challenged, were indeed some of the hardest
students to teach and potentially the riskiest to be recommended
for ministry.

Sarah Coakley explores these ideas with considerable sophistica-
tion in considering 'why is systematic theology distrusted?'[6] She
stresses the link of theological study, if it is to be done properly,
with contemplative and ascetic practice:

Theology is a *practical* discipline. It comes with the urge,
the fundamental desire, to seek God's face, and yet to have
that seeking constantly checked, corrected and purged . . .
Apophatic theology, in its proper sense . . . can never be mere
verbal play, deferral of meaning, or the simple addition of
negatives to positive ('kataphatic') claims. Nor on the other
hand can it be satisfied with the dogmatic 'liberal' denial
that God in Godself can be known *at all*: it is not 'mysterious' in *that* sense. For contemplation is the unique and
wholly *sui generis* task of seeking to know, and speak of
God, unknowingly; as Christian contemplation, it is also
the necessarily bodily practice of dispossession, humility
and effacement which, in the Spirit, causes us to learn

---

[5] Coleridge, S. T., *Aids to Reflection*, cited in Hardy, D. W., *God's Ways with the World*.
T & T Clark, Edinburgh, 1996, p. 174.
[6] Coakley, S., *God, Sexuality and the Self: An Essay 'On the Trinity'*. Cambridge University
Press, Cambridge, 2013, pp. 42–6.

incarnationally, and only so, the royal way of the Son to the Father.[7]

The integrated link between prayer, study and personal transformation is one reason that the Church of England has placed a high priority on periods of *residence* in theological education, whether this occurs at a college or on a course.[8] From a sociological perspective, powerful experiences of community have an important role in identity formation. We live in an age which is most deeply influenced by liberal individualism. But within such an outlook, one cannot begin to understand the nature of the Church, let alone the strongly communitarian understanding of personhood that is embodied in, for example, St Paul's teaching on 'the body of Christ'. In this context, it is entirely to be expected that for many people today, whether lay or ordained, their faith comes alive in some strong community context, whether a festival gathering, a church houseparty, or an experience of new monasticism.

And so to ordination

I was fortunate to be ordained both to the diaconate and to the presbyterate in the inspiring setting of Durham Cathedral. Since these ordinations, I have been a parish priest, taking ordination students on placement and training curates, taught in a theological college, worked as a vocations advisor and an assistant diocesan director of ordinands, and am now a bishop conducting ordinations myself. All of which has given me plenty of opportunity to think about the nature of ordination.

The first, and most important, ordination is into the *laos*, the people of God. Christian initiation in baptism – and especially

---

[7] Coakley, *God, Sexuality and the Self*, pp. 45–6.
[8] See, for example, ABM/ACCM, *Occasional Paper No. 38, Residence – An Education.* Church House, London, 1990.

confirmation (which were once all part of the same rite and in the Eastern Church still are) – involves a laying on of hands. To quote the Orthodox theologian John Zizioulas: 'It must be stated emphatically that there is no such a thing as "non-ordained" persons in the Church.'[9] The First Letter of Peter 2.9–10 heaps honorific titles upon the *laos*: 'But you are a chosen race, a royal priesthood, a holy nation, God's own people', for 'Once you were not a people, but now you are God's people [*laos theou*].' In this light, it would be a great pity if the Guidelines gave the impression that somehow the mission of the Church was 'mainly' the responsibility of one caste of people within it, namely the clergy.[10]

Ordination (as a deacon, priest or bishop) always occurs within the community of the Church, not apart from it. I am struck by a comment made by Stephen Platten in his book *Vocation* on the importance of the relational context:

> Vocation, then, is not simply a personal direct line to God, even though since the Reformation and Counter-Reformation it has often seemed so. Emphasis upon the individual's personal relationship with Christ emerged in both traditions and often submerged the truth that humanity is created and redeemed in solidarity and not only through individual lives . . . In recovering that sense of solidarity . . . vocation then needs to be seen rather differently. It now becomes an offering of an individual or individuals within the Church to see whether their particular talents, skills, character and abilities are such as to resonate with the vocation to which the whole of God's Church is called.[11]

---

[9] Zizioulas, J. D., *Being as Communion*. St Vladimir's Seminary Press, Crestwood NY, 1993, p. 215.

[10] Occasionally, there are hints of this attitude, for example when at the outset (1.1) the Guidelines assert that 'the three orders of ordained ministry play a central role in the mission of the Church which Jesus Christ entrusted to his Apostles to "go and make disciples of all the nations . . ."'.

[11] Platten, S., *Vocation*. SPCK, London, 2007, p. xiii.

As diocesan directors of ordinands know, some of the most difficult ordination candidates are those who feel their 'vocation' is a personal affair between them and God, which they must then persuade a reluctant Church to accept. It is the community that calls, and ministry is not a 'personal possession', nor a natural human right![12]

And to ministry

Ministry must be about relationships. That might sound pretty obvious, but this understanding has not always been the case. Within the Western tradition, debates about ordination and ministry started somewhere else. There were those who thought that ministry was mainly about a special grace given to someone in ordination, about a change that takes place in someone's soul to make them a priest (ontological views). Then there were others who thought ministry to be mainly about a set of functions – preaching, leading, caring and so on (functional views).

But in my experience neither of these views is adequate. The fundamental thing that changes when someone is ordained is their *relationship* with the Church and the Church's witness to the world. We become ambassadors for Christ in a strong, representational sense. We are regarded as pastors by our congregations. We represent and lead our community in its central acts of worship. This applies equally whether our community is the resident community of a parish, the constrained community of a prison, the temporary community of a hospital or the military community on a ship or base.[13] As a result of our relational position, yes, we do pick up a series of functions and responsibilities. More than that, *because my identity as a person depends on my relationships*, it is true to

---

[12] Helpful pastoral guidelines for beginning to address these often very painful situations are given in Thorp, H., *When the Church Says No*. Grove Books, Cambridge, 2004.

[13] For a wide-ranging account of ministry in chaplaincy and sector positions, see Threlfall-Holmes, M. and Newitt, M., *Being a Chaplain*. SPCK, London, 2011.

say that I do become a different person. I am changed. But the fundamental thing is our relationship with the ecclesial community.[14] We start to sense intuitively its joys and pains, we hold its tensions, we start to embody its identity. That of course is a great privilege and sometimes a costly burden.

This sense of public representation, and the accountability that goes with it, changes dramatically the moment someone is ordained. All kinds of minor indiscretions, poor judgements, personal peccadillos (not to say the major ones), start to matter a whole lot more both in the eyes of the Church and in the view of the public. This is one important reason why the clergy need to produce guidelines written for themselves and by themselves. Wider society remains deeply confused as to what is acceptable and what is not, not only for itself but for others. The Guidelines flesh out the hopes and expectations placed upon clergy by clergy and in so doing provide an enduring, creative framework for life and ministry.

Faith and dealing with its possible erosion

Throughout Christian history, spiritual authors have linked the love of God to the knowledge of God in a virtuous circle. The more we know God, the more we love God, and the more we love God the more we know God. Life 'in the Spirit' is life lived within this circle – being drawn more closely into the life of the triune God.

One might hope and expect that the life of the ordained minister would facilitate and stimulate this kind of growth. After all, the clergy are paid to pray and paid to study! In fact, 'staying fresh' theologically and spiritually is a major challenge. Stephen Covey has famously written of the importance of 'sharpening the saw' (see Chapter 7). The image is powerful: cutting wood with blunt

---

[14] This is rigorously explained in Zizioulas, *Being as Communion*, especially Chapter 6, 'Ministry and Communion'.

tools is not only hard work but can be dangerous. Interestingly, two of the four elements of Covey's saw sharpening are study and prayer (the other two relate to physical health and social/ emotional needs).[15]

The vicissitudes of life and the demands of ministry can and do grind clergy down. The causes of clergy stress and distress are legion and include: family and relationship problems, health issues, isolation and loneliness, addiction, financial difficulties, bullying from powerful parishioners, excessive pastoral workloads. In some cases clergy lose their 'first love' and the sense of calling they once had leaves them. There are those whose faith ebbs away or is broken by crisis, and who need to be ministered to, rather than be ministering to others.

All professions that involve caring for people are prone to induce cynicism in their practitioners after many years of service. But clergy have the added burden that they must declare week by week a faith in which they themselves must be living and growing if their proclamation is going to carry authenticity and conviction. For this reason, the Guidelines are realistic about ministers who find they are unable any longer in conscience to believe, hold or teach the Christian faith as the Church of England has received it, recommending they 'should seek advice and help in deciding whether or not they should continue to exercise a public ministry in which they represent the Church' (section 8.3).

It is tragic when the only thing keeping a minister in a post is the money – be it present income or future pension. Here any sense of calling or vocation is lost. The challenge is to find practical schemes for counselling into alternative occupations or for enabling retirement – for the benefit of all. I have been particularly impressed by the actions of certain former colleagues in such situations. One was unable to find a suitable new post and worked

---

[15] Covey, S. R., *The Seven Habits of Highly Effective People: Powerful Lessons in Personal Change*. Free Press, New York, 1989.

for a year as a delivery driver for IKEA, a second simply felt the need for a change of occupation and decided to retrain as an estate agent, and a third, who felt 'burnt out' after a long and effective ministry, started an antiques business in retirement. God's call upon our lives does not depend upon maintaining an ordained role, and there is more to life than working for the Church.

Conclusion

It is a basic Christian conviction that God speaks to his people.[16] Interpreting and living within his call to us is a life project.[17] The fundamental calling is to membership of the people of God. Within the community of the Church, some are called to the ordained roles of deacon, priest or bishop. These callings profoundly change our relationship with the Church, making us public representatives of the community. The Church rightly takes especial care to discern these callings and then to train its leaders for their roles.

Initial formation in community, with prayer and study, offers to men and women the possibility of developing leadership gifts and habits of lifelong learning and personal growth. In fulfilling their ordination vows, they carry the expectations and burdens of many. The Guidelines should not be understood as a rigid code of practice seeking to defend the position of an elite professional group, nor a text to undermine a vocation. They are there to clarify the high expectations placed on the Church's public representatives at a time when trust in leaders of all kinds is subject to deep questioning. And they are there to encourage and deepen that sense of calling and believing which is such an integral part of ordained ministry.

---

[16] Wolterstorff, N., *Divine Discourse*. Cambridge University Press, Cambridge, 1995, gives a philosophical defence of the claim that God could speak to us, most especially through Scripture.

[17] For some practical tips on how we can discern God's voice, see Shaw, P., *Deciding Well*. Regent College Publishing, Vancouver, 2009.

References

ABM/ACCM, *Occasional Paper No. 38, Residence – An Education*. Church House Publishing, London, 1990.

Coakley, S., *God, Sexuality and the Self: An Essay 'On the Trinity'*. Cambridge University Press, Cambridge, 2013.

Covey, S. R., *The Seven Habits of Highly Effective People: Powerful Lessons in Personal Change*. Free Press, New York, 1989.

Hardy, D. W., *God's Ways with the World*. T & T Clark, Edinburgh, 1996.

Harrison, J., Innes, R. and van Zwanenberg, T. (eds), *Rebuilding Trust in Healthcare*. Radcliffe Medical Press, Oxford, 2003.

O'Neill, O., *A Question of Trust*. Cambridge University Press, Cambridge, 2002.

Platten, S., *Vocation*. SPCK, London, 2007.

Shaw, G. B., *The Doctor's Dilemma*. Penguin, New York, 1946.

Shaw, P., *Deciding Well*. Regent College Publishing, Vancouver, 2009.

Thorp, H., *When the Church Says No*. Grove Books, Cambridge, 2004.

Threlfall-Holmes, M. and Newitt, M., *Being a Chaplain*. SPCK, London, 2011.

Wolterstorff, N., *Divine Discourse*. Cambridge University Press, Cambridge, 1995.

Zizioulas, J. D., *Being as Communion*. St Vladimir's Seminary Press, Crestwood NY, 1993.

Part 2
THE GUIDELINES
IN ACTION

4

Staying safe

PAUL BUTLER

Priests are called to be servants and shepherds among the people to whom they are sent. (The Ordinal)

Safeguarding is everyone's responsibility.
(*Working Together to Safeguard Children*)

The challenge to the Church

Any analysis of the newly revised set of Guidelines reveals that the most wide-ranging changes are in relation to safeguarding. Since the first Guidelines[1] were produced not only has the Church of England itself produced new policies, all of which will be revised again in 2016, but the whole cultural setting has been transformed. The Jimmy Savile case[2] is the most notorious public one but within the Church itself there have been significant issues relating to non-recent abuse[3] going back into the 1950s and ongoing challenges to be an ever safer church now. We live in a society that

---

[1] The Convocations of Canterbury and York, *Guidelines for the Professional Conduct of the Clergy*. Church House Publishing, London, 2003. The revision was published in 2015.

[2] Gov.uk., *NHS and Department of Health investigations into Jimmy Savile*. Department of Health, London, 2014. <https://www.gov.uk/government/collections/nhs-and-department-of-health-investigations-into-jimmy-savile>

[3] The term historical or historic abuse is often used to describe cases where the abuse happened in the past. The term is problematic for the victims and survivors of such abuse as while the event may have happened in the past the person still lives with the memory and impact of the abuse; it is thus not past but current. The term 'non-recent abuse' is that agreed to be used by the Goddard Inquiry to try and better define such cases.

is trying to come to terms with the reality of how widely abuse has happened. The home and family remain the primary place where abuse occurs; child abuse and domestic violence happen in each and every social stratum. But it is child sexual abuse in institutions like schools, hospitals, politics and the Church that has led to the National Inquiry led by Justice Lowell Goddard.[4]

The Church faces a particular set of challenges. We want to be welcoming to all. So we welcome and want to care for those who have been abused in contexts other than the Church. We want to be able to welcome those abused by members of our own institution; this requires our humility and repentance. We want to be welcoming to those who have perpetrated abuse. And, at the same time, we are incensed by abuse of every kind.

The Goddard Inquiry will focus specifically on child sexual abuse, and understandably this is particularly disturbing. It is criminal; it is sinful. But we are to be concerned with abuse in all its forms, whether sexual, physical, neglect, emotional or spiritual; and to respond to the abuse of people of all ages. There is something particularly heinous about child abuse; yet elder abuse, and abuse of adults when they are vulnerable, must also be of prime concern. Somehow we have to balance the potentially competing needs, interests and requirements of survivors and perpetrators of abuse, while ensuring that our churches remain safe places for all. It falls particularly to the clergy to lead churches into being such communities. So the responsibility on clergy is great.

Pastoral care

The Guidelines make it clear that it is in the context of the clergy's pastoral care that safeguarding must take place. So section 2, 'Care', makes a significant number of points about how clergy must develop awareness of their own limits and competences (2.3); the

---

[4] IICSA, *Independent Inquiry into Child Sexual Abuse*, London, 2015–.

need to give careful thought to how to go about pastoral visiting, including record-keeping (2.7) and how to think through specific matters like dress, lighting and seating arrangements, so that those for whom they care feel, and are, safe. The importance of training in safeguarding and safe practice is also made explicit in 2.11, alongside the need for a clear knowledge of policies and procedures, such as those to do with reporting.

There is reference to behaviour in relation to exposure to unwholesome materials (2.17). The growing issue of internet pornography in our society is one about which we probably do not speak enough. Sadly there are clergy who have been very seriously affected by their exposure to such material, including some who have downloaded images of child pornography, and thus contributed to the abuse of children.

So pastoral care includes what clergy offer to others, the proper care of themselves, and the oversight they provide for the church(es) for which they hold responsibility. There is information to be known, understood and held, and there are practices to follow. Alongside this is the need to recognize that clergy are not safeguarding professionals, so there must be a willingness in humility to seek advice from the Diocesan Safeguarding Adviser and, on occasions, other safeguarding professionals. The primary role of clergy remains to offer appropriate high-quality pastoral care, in a way that is safe for all.

Power and trust

It is within this framework that very particular consideration must be given to the issues of power and trust. As 2.4 puts it, 'Clergy should always be conscious of the power dynamics involved in their pastoral care, noting both the position of trust which they hold and the power which they exercise.' Francis Bridger's very insightful and helpful theological reflection picks this up especially clearly: 'Within the relationship between clergy and parishioners, it is crucial to appreciate that power is used asymmetrically. That is to say, the clergyman or woman is more powerful than the person seeking help.'[5] Section 12 also explores the issue of trust (see Chapter 11).

Imbalances of power, and questions of trust, are often poorly recognized or understood by clergy and their parishioners. Too often clergy are unaware that their position, their dress (the power of the collar and of robes) and their perceived special relationship with God, mean that, all too often, they are invested with both power and authority by those seeking their help and guidance. Even with the breakdown of confidence and trust in institutions it remains the case that clergy are invested with a great deal of trust. It is assumed that confidences will be held, that care will be taken, that words will be listened to and hidden messages heard. This can prove difficult for clergy. Some want to emphasize that they are part of the *laos*, the whole people of God, and therefore tend to dress down and operate in a relaxed style. Others see importance in being distinctive, wearing collar, black and cassock. The relaxed priest or deacon may misread how much trust is being placed in them, or how much power emanates from them. The more formal priest can equally misread that the 'cloaking' of the person they seek may not fully hide how much power their persona expresses.

Clergy are deeply trusted in their teaching, worship leading and pastoral roles. The very nature of the ministry they exercise exudes power and invites trust. It is essential for a safe church that clergy are deeply aware and conscious of these realities. A failure to recognize them can lead to all kinds of trouble, where people invest much more hope and confidence in the clergyperson than is realistic, leading to disappointment and disillusionment. It can equally lead to infatuation and attention, which, without due care, can lead to very unhelpful relationships.

---

[5] Bridger, F., 'A theological reflection' in *Guidelines for the Professional Conduct of the Clergy 2015, Revised edition*. Church House Publishing, London, 2015.

Clergy need to recognize their own need to be liked and wanted, and to recognize the temptations that can come with loneliness, tiredness and pressure. No clergyperson should ever say, 'It will never happen to me.' Affairs, and abusive relationships, happen to clergy. There is often failure to recognize the place that trust and power, or rather the misuse of trust and power, play in these events. So for healthy safeguarding, healthy self-care is important, as outlined in sections 13 (Well-being) and 14 (Care for the Carers).

Equally, the recognition that such power relationships can and do exist may lead the clergyperson to become over-anxious and cautious, and so fail to offer the help being sought for fear of getting it wrong. Awareness should lead to the wise exercise of power, not the avoidance of its use. There is a God-given authority to be used rightly by clergy; a failure to do so is to fail to fulfil a God-given calling.

More disturbingly, an awareness of how power and trust might operate may lead to their misuse and abuse. Clergy are in a position to be able to groom people and so exercise unhelpful power over them, leading to an individual being sexually or emotionally abused. Whole congregations can also be affected by the misuse of power. This form of spiritual abuse must be named and confronted. Once abusive power has been used it can later be exerted to make people fearful of challenging the clergyperson, or of disclosure to others. Clergy have to be aware of their own capacity to groom others, both individuals and congregations, as well as be aware of how others might groom them and their congregation.

The confessional

Clergy are called to a ministry of reconciliation. This is particularly about reconciliation between people and God, which must lead on to reconciliation between people too. Within this context sits the specific ministry of absolution. Priests pronounce absolution publicly with the declaration of God's forgiveness after corporate confession. But there is also the very specific ministry of absolution in the context of the confessional. The Guidelines offer a clear outline of what the current position is: absolute confidentiality within the bounds of the confessional remains. However, the Guidelines helpfully make it clear that within the context of a serious crime, such as abuse of children or vulnerable adults, the priest hearing the confession should require the penitent abuser to report this to the proper authority. If this is not done then absolution should be withheld (3.6).

This ought to give greater confidence that the confessional is not being used as a way to cover up abuse or, even worse, being used to allow further abuse to take place. However, there remains deep concern that such misuse and abuse of the confessional has happened, and continues to do so. Hence the *Guidelines* publication includes *GS Misc 1085*,[6] outlining the work that is being undertaken to explore whether or not the provisions of the relevant Canon (which dates from 1603) should be revised. The debate is not as simple as some suggest. It may well be that the existence of the confessional has helped some abusers to come forward and face up to their crimes in a way that they might not otherwise have done. For now, care must be taken to use this practice very carefully, noting in particular the requirement for repentance to be genuine, shown by confession to the relevant authorities and not only to the priest, before absolution is given.

Conclusion

Safeguarding children and adults is a gospel imperative because it is about the well-being of every human being. Jesus came to

---

[6] General Synod, *Guidelines for the Professional Conduct of the Clergy. The Ministry of Absolution. GS misc 1085*. Church House Publishing, London, 2014, <https://www.churchofengland.org/media/2101309/gs%20misc%201085%20-%20guidelines%20for%20the%20professional%20conduct%20of%20the%20clergy.pdf>. It should be noted that Section 3: Reconciliation, as printed in the Appendix to this book, reflects the current legal position in 2015 in relation to the ministry of absolution, which, as noted above, is under review.

give life in all its fullness; abuse of every kind takes that fullness away. Safeguarding is about how we behave individually and corporately towards one another so that everyone, of whatever age and however vulnerable or powerful, is treated with the dignity they deserve – as a person made in the image of God, and for whom Jesus Christ lived among us, died for us and rose again. Safeguarding therefore should not be seen as just a necessary hurdle to be jumped. Training should not be approached with unwillingness or cynicism. Disclosure and barring checks should not be viewed as an awkward administrative issue.

Safeguarding should be recognized as something healthy, part of recognizing frail humanity and longing for the creation of communities of Christ that are safe for all. Clergy have a pivotal role in the creation of such safe communities. They set the vision and the tone. As they exercise their power following in the way of Christ, as servants of all, they build communities of trust in which everyone can flourish. There is nowhere safer in all of creation than the arms of the God who made us and loves us. May all clergy reflect and make known in their words and their practice that 'safe place for all'.

References

The Convocations of Canterbury and York, *Guidelines for the Professional Conduct of the Clergy*. Church House Publishing, London, 2003, and *Revised edition*, 2015.

General Synod, *Guidelines for the Professional Conduct of the Clergy. The Ministry of Absolution. GS misc 1085*. Church House Publishing, London, 2014.

HM Government, *Working Together to Safeguard Children: A Guide to Inter-agency Working to Safeguard and Promote the Welfare of Children*. Government publications, London, 2015.

5

Embodying witness

JAMIE HARRISON

They are to tell the story of God's love.   (The Ordinal)

You are not the good news and you *are* the good news.
(Rowan Williams, Ascension Day 2015)

With these words, Archbishop Rowan provoked two new bishops
at their consecration service in Westminster Abbey – one can only
hope that they were both suitably inspired and chastened. I
certainly was. For being a witness, for good or ill, is unavoidable
as a Christian, whether ordained or lay. It goes with the territory.

I was reminded of this more than once as a GP who also
appeared on occasions as a blue-scarfed Reader. There were the
obvious comments on a home visit – 'Doctor, have you come to
cure or to bury today?' How did I come across? And what about
those grumpy times – 'No, you can't have an antibiotic!' Or, when
cross about 'being messed about', as I saw it, by folk who were
doubtless anxious and distressed by their symptoms, or those
of their loved ones. How easy it is to mount the high horse
until, of course, it throws you off. Bearing witness is challenge and
opportunity. It is non-negotiable. 'You will be my witnesses,' Jesus
says (Acts 1.8), whether we like it or not – witnesses in Carlisle
and Colchester, Berwick and Brighton; in the pub, at the school
gate, at the supermarket checkout, as well as in the church porch
and pulpit. And people notice.

For both family doctors and clergy, the public–private worlds
struggle to differentiate: less so for GPs who, increasingly, live

out of patch, unlike parish clergy. I still remember a much-loved ex-missionary GP partner, taken shopping by his wife, hiding behind the menswear stands in M&S to avoid contact with an approaching patient. The store was 20 miles from the practice! We can each tell similar stories. Yet deep inside we yearn to be those who witness well, who fly the flag, who stay 'corporate' and don't let the side down (whatever that means). If only we could do it better.

Responsive witness

Chris Russell, in his playful book *Ten Letters*, imagines letters he is writing to particular friends after his own death. He explores the influence his own witness might have had on them, and shapes responses to their questions and beliefs. He wants to draw them into reflecting on what really matters, and to offer signposts for their futures; his own ability to signpost (as a witness) being now at an end following his fictional demise. As the Archbishop of Canterbury's Adviser on Evangelism and Witness, Chris also offers insights into how a city-centre church (in Reading, in his case) might engage with significant numbers of young people without turning into a youth church. Older Christians get involved, engaging in worship, music and mentoring. Over the last 12 years, the church has attracted large numbers of youngsters, seeking to nurture and support them. Yet, when asked by the local bishop, 'How many have you baptized this year?', the answer proved to be a disappointing 'three'.

Karl Barth called the Church to be 'a witness of, and to, Jesus Christ'.[1] In this Chris and his church had done well, much better than most of the rest of us, in terms of contacts and conversations with young people, providing safe and supportive places in which

---

[1] Barth, K., *Church Dogmatics IV.3, Second Half*. T & T Clark, Edinburgh, 1962, pp. 554–613.

to be. But they had not seen the fruit for which they had hoped and prayed. So they began to use weekends away, and saw a number of young people come to a living faith. Weekends give space and time to talk and connect. They also brought their focus to bear on fewer activities, but in more depth. In this they enriched their relationships and deepened their connections. What had been merely contact and nurture became commitment and growth, all in the context of faithful witness and a call to discipleship. And more came forward for baptism.

Barth's call to be a witness of, and to, Jesus Christ invites us all to find ways of telling our own stories of faith. Chris insisted that his job title had the word 'witness' in it. While 'not every Christian is an evangelist', we are all witnesses to Jesus, good or bad, whether we realize it or not, if we claim to follow him. For 'in Jesus Christ, God has truly turned towards us' and so 'everyone is a witness' and this becomes our vocation.

Authentic witness

There are those who warn that no one should endorse a product that they themselves do not use – unlike certain celebrities. People, particularly younger folk, see through insincerity and value what is true and authentic. Where witness is honest and holistic – at home, in the street, with friends and neighbours, and in church – such witness provokes others to ask questions and seek answers. Conversations will be about doubt, uncertainty, failure and difficulty, as much as about joy and hope. The New Testament uses the same Greek word for 'witness' and 'martyr'; there will be a cost in being a faithful witness. Christians follow the Way of the cross. Dietrich Bonhoeffer lived out that reality, noting in his book *Discipleship* that the call of Christ is a call that leads us to death.[2]

---

[2] Bonhoeffer, D., *Discipleship*. Fortress Press, Minneapolis MN, 2003, p. 81.

So it is right to emphasize the physicality and integrity of authentic witness, the embodiment of following the Way. Hiding or denying brokenness and vulnerability, just as much as failing to express confidence and elation, goes against the integration of a humanity made new in Jesus Christ. If C. S. Lewis was willing to speak of being surprised by joy, he was also prepared to write about a grief observed. For Lewis, the 'problem of pain' only became fully real when he was touched by it personally, and his witness in his later writings gains from that perspective – or perhaps it was only through that later grief that he could finally release the pain that he had held deep inside since his beloved mother's death from cancer when he was aged only nine. Part of witnessing well is to know yourself better.

Lewis the popular apologist also moved from using traditional academic means (he was, after all, a major literary scholar) to narrative and fantasy, not least in the world of children's literature. Some see this as a retreat following his 'defeat' in the Oxford debate featuring the Roman Catholic philosopher Elizabeth Anscombe. Others see it as a natural progression, a harking back to earlier influences, not least the fantasy world of George MacDonald and the (re-)discovery of a new way of writing. Equally, one might see, in what Rowan Williams writes of as *The Lion's World*, a heaven-given opportunity to flesh out an author's living faith in unexpected ways (Lewis always denied any apologetic intention), an outflowing of creativity. Lewis believed that his books would quickly disappear from view after his death and that he would be soon forgotten. He realized neither the quality of his work nor that later generations would respond better to narrative and story than to argument and the voice of the academy. His Christian witness, popularity and focus on apologetics all worked against his gaining proper academic recognition until he received a Cambridge professorship at the age of 56.

Witness in dialogue

For Lesslie Newbigin, the congregation acts as 'the hermeneutic of the gospel'.[3] Again we would want to see words backed up by integrity – what you see is what you get; what is written on the tin is what is contained inside; slice through it and it stays constant and consistent. Yet, a focus on hermeneutics also calls on the idea of interpretation – what does it mean and how does it work? It's a two-way street, and as I engage with the world so it engages back with me, and together we enter into a dialogue which allows both parties to make sense of each other. And here the 'world' may be the family next door. Equally, in a pluralistic world, this must include engaging in dialogue with people of different religions and cultures (see Acts 17.22–28).

Seen in this light, witness cannot just be viewed as carrying a placard saying 'Jesus loves you', true and worthy as that might be. Indeed, in some places such a placard could lead to imprisonment and even death. The call to dialogue is shaped by context and by our behaviour, as much as by our listening and our telling. The Ordinal quotation at the top of this chapter calls on clergy 'to tell the story of God's love'. Yet telling can only make sense in the act of giving and receiving, of being and of becoming. The Guideline on 'mission', to which this chapter is a response, speaks of 'the cure of souls', of baptizing, of thoughtful preparation and of ensuring that 'appropriate and accessible courses and discussion groups on all aspects of the Christian faith are available at regular intervals to parishioners seeking to explore, deepen or renew their faith'. The importance of schools is also noted – places of learning and of social formation. The emphasis is on ministry, mission and evangelism; but these will only be fruitful, it seems to me, where there is true dialogue in a spirit of humble active listening.

[3] Newbigin, L., *The Gospel in a Pluralist Society.* Eerdmans/World Council of Churches, Grand Rapids MI and Geneva, 1989, pp. 222–33.

In the chapter 'Speaking the Truth to Caesar', Newbigin is clear that any serious commitment to evangelism must be accompanied by a radical questioning of the reigning assumptions of public life.[4] In other words, to be serious requires not only naming our own intentions, prejudices, assumptions, myths and fantasies, but also leaving behind these preoccupations to be able to critique the external public world in which we find ourselves. Clergy in particular are those called to 'tell the story of God's love', which can be both good news and not good news, to echo the words of Rowan Williams quoted earlier. An important recent example of this was the publication of *On Rock or Sand?*,[5] which considered the values needed to build a just and compassionate society, while also offering a robust critique of current inequalities. Clergy are tasked to proclaim with wisdom. In telling the story of the gospel, good news for the poor may not be such good news for the rich, as the Magnificat reminds us.[6] Faithful witnesses will live with their own acknowledged failings in the search for dialogue and the possibility of change and renewal in the wider community to which they are called and of which they are also a part.

And, notably, in that ancient world of Caesar, Michael Green reminds us that most first- and second-century Christians came to faith through their friends and neighbours, sharing what they believed, within families, at markets, city gates . . . not through the high-profile preaching of famous people like St Paul.[7]

When witness disappoints

Too often the experience both inside and outside the Church is that of disappointment – of what might have been, of hopes dashed,

[4] Newbigin, L., *Truth to Tell. The Gospel as Public Truth*. SPCK, London, 1991, pp. 65–90.
[5] Sentamu, J. (ed.), *On Rock or Sand?*. SPCK, London, 2015.
[6] Luke 1.46–55.
[7] Green, M., *Evangelism in the Early Church*. Hodder & Stoughton, London, 1973, pp. 207–18, 278–80.

of possibilities lost. People we trusted let us down, promises were broken, relationships fractured. It was 'such a bad witness', we might say. And those who have suffered particular hurts and failures struggle to recover and forgive, and vow never to darken the church door again.

Motives matter in the detail and in the big picture. As Gandhi said, 'The moment there is suspicion about a person's motives, everything he does becomes tainted.' Elsewhere in this book, authors seek to address the issue of trust lost and trust regained – like trying to rethread a fractured spider's web, as Wittgenstein once put it. Where clergy (or I) are not good news, it may be our fault or just the way things are. In his chapter on leadership, Stephen Cherry reminds us that we can't please everyone all the time.[8] In his Ascension Day sermon, Rowan Williams reminded the soon-to-be-ordained bishops that they would be too bold in some decisions and too timid in others; that they would be misunderstood, as well as getting it wrong, on occasions.

And, in other ways, we may not, at first glance, seem to be the good news. Witness is frequently about people testifying to the love of Jesus in the messiness and brokenness of their own situations – which may seem far from being good news. As is often said, 'Evangelism is one beggar telling another beggar where to find bread.' Lay people, as well as clergy, are indispensable in this. It is about being able to get alongside someone else that counts, about being vulnerable, and about being honest.

For faithful witness can only live in, and for, hope, and seek do its best 'to tell the story of God's love'. It is to that theme that the final section of this chapter turns. For Stanley Hauerwas, 'Witness names the truth that the only way we can know the character of the world, the only way we know ourselves, the only way we know God, is by one person telling another.'[9]

---

[8] See Chapter 7, 'Giving leadership', in this volume.
[9] Hauerwas, S., *Approaching the End. Eschatological Reflection on Church, Politics and Life.* SCM Press, London, 2014, p. 38.

Witness as wisdom

It is in the telling. The Apostle John grasped that Jesus was the Word and Wisdom of God, and set out to tell the world. That task has now been handed on to us. For clergy, the Ordinal is clear – preach the word, declare the mighty acts of God, baptize new disciples, nurture, preside, lead, offer praise and thanksgiving. Here, to witness is to live out a notable calling, and to do so much in the public gaze. There are few places to hide, and many traps into which to fall.

Perhaps there is comfort in knowing that laity, too, are caught in this, if perhaps to a less visible extent. 'The clergy should recognize, affirm and encourage the ministry and witness of lay people. This should include acknowledging their mission in work-places and communities,' as Guideline 4.5 puts it. Wisdom lies in knowing who we truly are, as those deeply loved by God, frail and imperfect though we may be. Wisdom speaks about knowing our limitations and not taking ourselves too seriously.

Wisdom also helps each of us, when called upon, to give an account of the hope that is within us, not in some formulaic or pious way, but in words and feelings that are truly our own and are gracious (1 Peter 3.15). The quality and nature of how we do that matters, and the ground-breaking joint statement *Christian Witness in a Multi-Religious World: Recommendations for Conduct* by the World Council of Churches, Roman Catholic Church and World Evangelical Alliance lays out clear ground rules for conduct. The statement reminds us of the privilege and joy of giving this account of our faith, doing so with gentleness and with respect. It reminds us that Jesus Christ is the 'supreme witness' and that Christian witness is always a sharing in his witness in proclamation of the good news, in service of neighbour and in the total giving of self. It is indeed a high and costly calling – to be a faithful witness to Jesus Christ.

The statement highlights the need for gracious witness in a pluralistic world, engaging in dialogue with people of different religions and cultures (cf. Acts 17.22–28). It notes the difficulty and cost of such witness, hindered or even prohibited as it may be. It warns against engaging in inappropriate methods, such as deception or coercion – means that betray the gospel and can cause suffering to others. And it affirms that, while Christians have a responsibility to witness to Jesus Christ, conversion is ultimately the work of the Holy Spirit (cf. John 16.7–9; Acts 10.44–47) and that, ultimately, the Spirit blows where the Spirit wills (John 3.8)!

I am indebted to Chris Russell and to Justin Welby for providing inspiration for this chapter, notably through Chris's presentation to the Diocesan Lay Chairs' Conference, and for Justin's Inaugural Lambeth Lecture, both given in March 2015 (the latter available on the Archbishop of Canterbury's website at <www.archbishopofcanterbury.org/articles.php/5515/lambeth-lectures-archbishop-justin-on-evangelism-video>).

References

Barth, K., *Church Dogmatics IV.3, Second Half.* T & T Clark, Edinburgh, 1962.
Bonhoeffer, D., *Discipleship.* Fortress Press, Minneapolis MN, 2003.
Green, M., *Evangelism in the Early Church.* Hodder & Stoughton, London, 1970.
Newbigin, L., *The Gospel in a Pluralist Society.* Eerdmans/World Council of Churches, Grand Rapids MI and Geneva, 1989.
Newbigin, L., *Truth to Tell. The Gospel as Public Truth.* SPCK, London, 1991.
Russell, C., *Ten Letters. To Be Delivered in the Event of My Death.* Darton, Longman & Todd, London, 2012.
Sentamu, J. (ed.) *On Rock or Sand?.* SPCK, London, 2015.
Williams, R., *The Lion's World. A Journey to the Heart of Narnia.* SPCK, London, 2012.
World Council of Churches, Pontifical Council for Interreligious Dialogue and World Evangelical Alliance, *Christian Witness in a Multi-Religious World: Recommendations for Conduct.* World Council of Churches, Geneva, 2011, and online at <www.worldea.org/index.php/news/3578>.

6

Offering blessing

———•◦•———

RUSS PARKER

They are to bless the people in God's name.

(The Ordinal)

Bless – that's your job, to bless.   (1 Peter 3.9, *The Message*)

Blessing is a tall order. The Ordinal explores the shape of the blessing the priest is to be among the congregation, all in the context of the need for health and healing: 'They are to resist evil, support the weak, defend the poor, and intercede for all in need. They are to minister to the sick and prepare the dying for their death.'[1]

For me, the word 'blessing' used to be about praying for God to answer my prayers and to do something good in someone's life. There were no specifics attached to praying 'Lord bless this person, Lord bless our church'. It was Christian shorthand asking God to do something or to bring well-being. Not a bad thing to desire, of course, but if we are honest with ourselves this kind of praying also comes with the hazard of becoming boring after a while, with an almost zero level of expectation.

The secular equivalent is the carte blanche use of the term that we find the world over. When someone sneezes we say, 'Bless you!' When a baby does something endearing we say, 'O how sweet. Bless!' And there are still a few would-be sons-in-law who ask the

---

[1] The Convocations of Canterbury and York, *Guidelines for the Professional Conduct of the Clergy, 2015, Revised edition.* 'Guideline 5, Ministry at times of deepest need.' Church House Publishing, London, 2015.

father of their intended bride for his consent, or his blessing. It all conveys the wish to see good fortune for someone, or is a way of saying 'thank you'.

However, the Bible teaches us that blessing is a unique ministry resource, gifted to both priest and lay alike, to bring about the purposes of God in peoples' lives. And, like any other ministry procedure, it has its own dynamics and rhythms of grace.

The word of blessing

The word 'blessing' has travelled a long distance in its meaning and it began in blood. It can be traced back to the Old Teutonic German *bletsian* which means blood. The *Shorter Oxford English Dictionary* suggests that it refers to an animal sacrifice or to someone marked with blood before being offered in ritual sacrifice. To summarize we can say that the original meaning of the word was costly blood sacrifice. In the course of time it was used to translate the Latin *benedicere*, and its Greek counterpart *eulogein*, 'to speak well of'. Consequently the term 'blessing' is embedded within themes of costliness, impartation of benefit, and celebration. Such meanings cohere well with the mission of Jesus, his saving life and death and his default position of celebrating our humanity and capacity for growth. Who else would see potential in a hated tax collector hiding in the thick foliage of a tree on the outskirts of town and remind his critics of his true identity, that he too is a son of Abraham (Luke 19.9)?

For Henri Nouwen, this concept of generous hospitality, of saving celebration, is fundamental. For him, 'Hospitality is not to change people, but to offer them space where change can take place.' Hospitality must never be tribal or partisan, nor about bringing others over to 'our side', but 'to offer freedom not disturbed by dividing lines'.[2]

---

[2] Nouwen, H., *Reaching Out: The Three Movements of the Spiritual Life.* Image Books, New York, 1986, p. 71.

Words of blessing matter. The priest's offering of such a word of God's blessing, whether in the context of sickness or of health, enables and resources others to know that they are children of God. 'Resisting evil', to quote the Ordinal, is a dismantling of the powers and the words that have bent them out of shape and that prevent holy growth. 'Supporting the weak' is for such time until they can take back responsibility for their lives again. 'Ministering to the sick', whether they recover or not, is to help them to continue in newness of life. 'Preparing the dying for their death' is to help them to stay connected to the truth that matters to them, as they let go of many things. Granted, we do not win all the time, nor achieve all our goals; but we are in good company because Jesus had his losses too.

Old Testament words of blessing

The Old Testament words for blessing are *barak* and *berakhah*, and they are both derived from the word for 'knee' (although the word is rarely used to refer to the physical act of kneeling). At their core the words mean to show respect, and this is often accompanied with bowing or kneeling. A good question to ask here is, 'Who is bowing the knee? Is it the one being blessed or the one giving the blessing?'

Entertain for the moment the concept of God bowing the knee. This does not mean that God is at the mercy of our demands and prayers, but rather illustrates the servant heart of God who longs to meet the needs of a broken creation. This is more than echoed in the actions of Jesus who summarized his whole ministry in the words, 'I am among you as one who serves' (Luke 22.27). The theme of servant slave is continued in the great hymn of Philippians 2.6–11. Consequently the ministry of blessing is to serve the need of the other to flourish in the way that God wills for them.

The *Theological Wordbook of the Old Testament* states that 'to bless means to endue with power for success, prosperity and fecundity and longevity'.[3] I confess that I have problems with prosperity, not least when linked to an easy 'get-rich-quick' form of Christianity. I much prefer the concept of flourishing. This implies growth and fulfilment – in being the full-blown version of myself that God created me to be. It also means living well and walking in newness of life. It is this that forms the core of Christian healing. We still have to live well, whether we have been cured or not, whether we remain with the sickness we would rather do without or whether we are facing the ending of things. After all, we have met many very 'healthy' people who are not flourishing or walking in newness of life with God.

I well remember Colin Urquhart, one of the pioneers of the Charismatic Movement in the twentieth century, sharing an experience he had during a week-long healing and renewal mission he led. Every night, at the end of his talk, Colin would invite people to come forward for prayer for healing with the laying on of hands or to come and join the team in praying for others if they wished. After a few evenings, an angry man in a wheelchair rammed the wheels of his chair into Colin's legs causing him to wince with pain. He spoke out, saying that when the invitation was given to come for prayer or to join the team, he came forward to join the team. However, because he was in a wheelchair, Colin's team automatically assumed he was coming forward to receive prayer. The man declared, 'As far as I am concerned I am whole and well in my life and I want to serve. Why can't you see that?'

New Testament words of blessing

There are two New Testament words relating to blessing, *eulogia* and *makarios*. The first describes the powerful effects of consecrated speech and the second is a description or status of those who are blessed.

---

[3] Harris, Laird H., *Theological Wordbook of the Old Testament*, Vol. 1. Moody Press, Chicago IL, 1980, p. 132.

Eulogia sounds very much like the English word eulogy. A cynical definition of this I once heard was 'the lies we tell about people at their funerals'! I well remember attending the funeral of my great-aunt Rosie and listening to her being described as an inspiration of virtue and gentleness. However, this didn't sound at all like the Rosie I knew, who was both wild and caring and battled with a heavy alcohol regime. Granted that funerals are not the place to list the misdemeanours of the deceased, but I think her family felt robbed that day. Therefore to bless is not to offer flattery or well-meaning platitudes or wish-fulfilments. It is much more serious than this. A working definition of *eulogia* is 'to speak "well words" so that you will flourish in the way that God has called you'.

We also find the word *eulogia* used in the Greek Old Testament, the Septuagint, translating the Hebrew word *barak* on over 400 occasions. We see its use in what is perhaps the best-known blessing in the Bible – the Aaronic blessing in the book of Numbers:

> The LORD bless you and keep you;
> the LORD make his face to shine upon you,
>   and be gracious to you;
> the LORD lift up his countenance upon you,
>   and give you peace.   (Numbers 6.24–26)

Notice here that we find a pronouncement of blessing rather than a request, conveying an authority and an expectation of God-given outcome. Indeed, we are informed of the expected outcome. 'So they shall put my name on the Israelites, and I will bless them' (Numbers 6.27). This relates to the fact that the Israelite community, as the people of God, had reneged on its covenant commitment in the debacle of the golden calf: they were in danger of losing their identity. The blessing pronouncement was to signal their return to being a community of faith, one carried by the presence and power of God.

This blessing prayer also emphasizes that it is God who blesses. The challenge for those who serve as priests to their parish's need is to give space and time to listen to God for the content and focus of the words of blessing they are called to pronounce. Such appropriate words may also help to determine how to come alongside others, as an incarnation of that blessing. Thankfully as priests we do not do this alone but are commissioned to encourage a vital lay participation in mission and ministry.

Blessing from weakness

Barbara Brown Taylor, in her book *An Altar in the World*, relates the events surrounding the death of her father, caused by his advanced brain cancer, two weeks before one Christmas Day. He had had a seizure and was urgently admitted to hospital. A range of family members followed by car, and the small emergency room cubicle was rapidly filled to overflowing with anxious relatives. At one point, Barbara recounts, her husband Ed left her side to kneel down by her father's bed, saying something into his ear and holding the father's hand firmly on his own head. Ed remained still for a moment, while words were spoken over him, and he then got up.

> 'What was that?' I asked when he came back to slump beside me again. 'I asked him to bless me,' Ed said. 'I asked him to give me his blessing.'[4]

Taylor goes on to explain that this kind of blessing prayer is a form of benediction. It comes at the end of something, to send someone on their way. I love the reverse polarity of the story, and how it underlines that, in weakness, we can still give our gifts away, that others may grow. The experience transformed and revolutionized Taylor's understanding of blessing, opening up for her the possibility that anyone can do this – all can ask and all can bless, something the world needs and needs us to do

---

[4] Taylor, B. B., *An Altar in the World: Finding the Sacred Beneath Our Feet*. Canterbury Press, Norwich, 2009, pp. 207–8.

because there is a real shortage of people willing to kneel wherever they are and recognize the holiness holding its sometimes bony hand, often tender, always life-giving hand above their heads . . . That we are willing to bless one another is miracle enough to stagger the very stars.[5]

The call to bless takes on many guises, as I have found on my own journey, not least when writing *Rediscovering the Ministry of Blessing*. I was recently greatly encouraged by the way Mike Cosser has been challenged to bless the shops and businesses in the shopping complex near to where he lives in the East Midlands.[6] Wisely, he thought carefully before proceeding, and worked out a simple strategy, with a blessing prayer, to offer to the staff in those shops. He would first explain his purpose to the shop managers (that he would love the honour of blessing their shops) so that their businesses might perform a valuable service to the community. He then would show them the standard blessing below and ask permission to proceed.

> In the name of Jesus Christ, our Lord, we bless you with abundant trade in all seasons.
> We bless you and your staff that they may be skillful, knowledgeable, friendly, healthy, happy, and a real blessing on all the many customers that they encounter.
> May your goods and services be of good quality, great value and appreciated by your customers.
> We bless you with the favour of God in your business, and in your homes.
> Amen.

Needless to say, he had a mixed response. Some refused his offer, others were bemused, but many said yes and, in one example, the

---

[5] Taylor, *An Altar in the World*, pp. 208–9.
[6] Mike Cosser is a friend and businessman from Coventry. The quote is from a self-published document entitled 'A Blessing on this Local Business' and is used with permission.

entire staff of a supermarket lined up while he spoke out his blessing over them all.

Blessing from vulnerability

That second New Testament word, *makarios*, is almost exclusively used in reference to the Beatitudes, found in the Gospels of Matthew (5.3–12) and Luke (6.20–23). William Barclay, in his commentary on Matthew, says that the word 'blessed' is more of an exclamation than a statement and should therefore be translated 'O the blessedness of . . .'. He insists that the Beatitudes are congratulations in relation to what is now the experience of the blessed, even though these words of Jesus are given in the context of suffering and persecution.[7]

Tom Wright reflects that what Jesus offers in such beatitudes is an announcement, not a philosophical analysis of the world. While mourners may still go uncomforted, and those who long for justice may yet be unsatisfied, his kingdom work has now begun. 'It is *gospel*: good news, not good advice.'[8]

Barclay offered his own version of the Beatitudes, in order to tease out the nature of the experience of that blessed state to which he refers. For example, the poor in spirit become those who, in realizing their utter helplessness, and putting their whole trust in God, are able to render perfect obedience and so become citizens of heaven. In particular, I am struck very forcibly by his rendering of Matthew 5.7 and how it once again connects us with the Ordinal in describing the priest's commission to bless the people from the point of total engagement:

> 'Blessed are the merciful, for they will receive mercy.'
>
> (Matthew 5.7)

[7] Barclay, W., *The Gospel of Matthew, Vol.1: Daily Study Bible*. St Andrew Press, Edinburgh, 1972, p. 83.
[8] Wright, T., *Matthew for Everyone*. SPCK, London, 2002, p. 36.

O the bliss of those who can get right inside other people, until they can see with their eyes, think with their thoughts, feel with their feelings, for those who do that will find others do the same for them, and will know that that is what God in Christ Jesus has done.[9]

Far from blessing being a sort of benign and good-will presence to others, it means being vulnerable and empathic to the struggles and pain common to us all. Henri Nouwen, in his book *The Wounded Healer*, links it with the necessary stance of the priest, not hiding but owning his or her own weaknesses, so that they become an invitation for others to connect and thus create the community of the faithful. This is the context in which healing can begin, where 'mutual confession then becomes a mutual deepening of hope, and sharing weakness becomes a reminder to one and all of coming strength'.[10]

Conclusion

The commission to be the people that bless is a call to walk alongside, and be a companion to, those who struggle with life's tricks and tragedies. It is a call to walk alongside our own vulnerability and needs and to be brave enough to make them the place where we invite others in. It is the call to listen well, because at least once in every person's lifetime they will need to tell their story and know that they have been heard. It is the call to pronounce with expectation those 'well words' that invite the God of grace to respond and empower others to flourish in the way that God wants for them. It is the call to believe, often against the odds, that our words and deeds of blessing will make a difference and that even in the dark we shall be Christ among us.

[9] Barclay, W., *The Plain Man Looks at the Beatitudes.* Collins Fount Paperback, London, 1978, p. 68.

[10] Nouwen, H., *The Wounded Healer.* Darton, Longman & Todd, London, 1994, p. 94.

I would like to close with an excerpt from Stewart Henderson's poem 'Priestly duties', which I find very appropriate as we seek to be the people who bless.

> So, what does a priest do? . . .
> visits hospices, administers comfort,
> conducts weddings, christenings –
> not necessarily in that order,
> takes funerals,
> consecrates the elderly to the grave,
> buries children and babies,
> feels completely helpless beside
> the swaying family of a suicide.
>
> What does a priest do?
> Tries to colour in God . . .[11]

References

Barclay, W., *The Gospel of Matthew, Vol.1: Daily Study Bible*. St Andrew Press, Edinburgh, 1972.

Henderson, S., 'Priestly duties', in *Limited Edition*. Plover Books, London, 1997.

Nouwen, H., *Reaching Out: The Three Movements of the Spiritual Life*. Image Books, New York, 1986.

Nouwen, H., *The Wounded Healer*. Darton, Longman & Todd, London, 1994.

Parker, R., *Rediscovering the Ministry of Blessing*. SPCK, London, 2014.

Shorter Oxford English Dictionary, 6th edn. Oxford University Press, Oxford, 2007.

Taylor, B. B., *An Altar in the World: Finding the Sacred Beneath Our Feet*. Canterbury Press, Norwich, 2009.

Wright, T., *Matthew for Everyone*. SPCK, London, 2002.

---

[11] Henderson, S., 'Priestly duties' (written for Eric Delve, 23.5.96), published in *Limited Edition*. Plover Books, London, 1997, p. 21. It is used in this form with permission. The full poem is printed at the beginning of this book.

7

Giving leadership

STEPHEN CHERRY

Guided by the Spirit, they are to discern and foster the gifts
of all God's people.   (The Ordinal)

The leader who imposes his or her own view reduces the
creative capacity of the group.
    (Christoph H. Loch, Judge Business School, Cambridge)

Living with the L-word

Let me share with you a micro-story that comes from the time
when I was a parish priest. It was an occasion of shame for me
when it happened, and I still feel a slightly uncomfortable emotional twang – might that be guilt? – when I recall it. It is this.
Sometimes, when in the town centre, or indeed if visiting a city,
I would pop into a bookshop and wander over, affecting a certain
nonchalance, to the 'business' section and have a browse at the
bright, shiny, encouraging, indeed often enthusiastic, leadership
and management books. I picked them from the shelves and
enjoyed the layout, the illustrations, the upbeat chapter titles and
the positive and amusing drop-quotes.

Theology had never been presented to me in such a positive
way! Indeed, theology books seemed to be pre-sprayed with dust
and designed with a view simply to get the maximum number of
words on a page and written by someone determined to win gold
at the Footnote Olympics. But these books were different. They

were brassy, bold and self-confident and their readers were going to change the world. I liked them.

But I really did feel guilty. 'Surely,' I thought, 'I shouldn't give my time, my mind, my heart, my imagination to this stuff. I am not into personal success or the desire to reap great rewards. I am into ministry. I have a parish to be vicar of, funerals to take, schools to support, a congregation to care for and develop, services to make more lively and engaging, babies to baptize, couples to marry, and, oh yes, a massive grade-1 listed building to save from the already manifest ravages of dry rot, and another one, just a quarter of a mile away, which is all too obviously surplus to requirements, but very much loved by the dozen octogenarians who attend it once a week. And I get irritated and annoyed when people on the finance committee say (and they did say) that "the church is business, we have to work within financial constraints and live within our means".'

Seven clichés adopted

One day, of course, I cracked. The browsing led to a purchase. Hiding it in a brown paper bag, I smuggled Steven Covey's *The Seven Habits of Highly Effective People* into the Rectory study and read it through, feeling both shame and disloyalty as I enjoyed the modest buzz that told me that I was getting answers to some of my questions here. But really, was it right that I should aspire to being 'highly effective'? Surely this was some kind of offence against the theology of grace that taught me that the last thing that mattered was 'work'. And yet, when I reviewed my day, not in a formal way, but maybe cycling home after a funeral visit and thinking about the dry rot in the church roof, I came to the realization that, 'hey, a lot of this *is* work'.

So, I read Stephen Covey from cover to cover. And maybe what happened was a conversion experience: *here* is a place of under-standing and *this* is a source of wisdom! Not about eternal truths, perhaps, but about getting stuff done. His simple axioms are, I now realize, well-worn clichés, but just because something is a cliché doesn't make it untrue. And so I do indeed always now try to 'begin with the end in mind', I naturally think of trust as something that needs to be built up rather than assumed, I know that time can't be managed but that I can organize myself better to work within temporal limits, and I am very enthusiastic for 'sharpening the saw' – that is, not keeping going relentlessly, but stopping both for rest and to make sure that the tools I am using are both the right ones and are in good order.

Covey's books got me going on all this sort of thing, and when in my next post I found myself responsible for continuing ministerial development of clergy I had a licence to indulge myself; not only acquiring lots of shiny optimistic books, but finding endless other sources of such wisdom. It was with a sense of pioneering enthusiasm that I set up professional coaching opportunities for clergy to help them manage themselves and their tasks, and subjected myself, very willingly, to the same process. I had learnt by now that management was not the same as leadership and that leadership was not the same thing as effectiveness either – no real need for a leader to read Covey – though someone in the system must! But I had also learnt to be wary of the 'L-word'.

I knew perfectly well that many if not most dioceses were setting up 'leadership programmes' and many were making participation an obligation. This, I felt, was a huge risk: better to help people discover their own need and desire to wise-up about some of this stuff and to point them in the direction of the literally millions of resources out there. My judgement was that just as most clergy had learnt at some point in their lives to drive cars and use computers without any intervention from their local CMD officer, so too would they learn how to be more effective at the 'work' that is almost invariably part and parcel of ordained ministry today once they realized that it was possible. I was also a bit suspicious of the L-word as I couldn't for the life of me see what it added to the idea of 'ministry', and, when I came across Robert Greenleaf's idea of servant leadership, I was even *less* convinced that here was anything new or to be emulated.

Servant leadership questioned

The whole point of ordination, it seemed to me, was to make it absolutely clear that authority and service were vested (almost literally, come to think of it) in the same person. Today I am less optimistic about thinking like this about the ordained, but have not warmed to the 'servant leadership' idea, which often comes across as a bit manipulative, banking that people will be more likely to go along with you if you have insisted on doing the washing-up after the bun fight than if you leave it to the people whose sense of purpose and participation depends on being able to do that sort of thing.

In fact, I have now come to the view that 'servant leadership' is at best a way of trying to articulate something of the humility that is necessary not to *leadership* per se, but to ministry, or, come to think of it, not necessary to ministry per se but to discipleship – and indeed it is hard for me to think of a really good and admirable person of any faith or in any walk of life who is devoid of the quality of humility. But humility is a difficult thing to discuss, a troublesome and unfashionable virtue to think about, and not at all the sort of subject you expect to read about in a glossy business leadership book.

Good to great and why Vanstone is wrong

Yet that's where you would be wrong. One of the ultimate all-time best-sellers in this genre is *Good to Great* by Jim Collins, who did a massive research project into the qualities of companies that had gone from being merely good to 'great' and sustained their success over a period of at least 15 years. It was through doing this research that Collins came up with the notion of five levels of leadership of which the top – Level Five – was the kind of leader that these great companies had.

There are three very interesting and relevant points to note from Collins' work. The first is that Collins had been convinced, before the research project, that leadership was not going to have been a key factor. 'In fact, I gave the research team explicit instructions to downplay the role of top executives so that we could avoid simplistic "credit the leader" or "blame the leader" thinking common today.'[1] Indeed he goes on to rubbish what he calls the 'leadership is the answer to everything' mentality that he sees as 'the modern equivalent of the "God is the answer to everything" perspective that held back our scientific understanding of the physical world in the Dark Ages'.

The second point is what the leadership in the great companies was *not* like. His list is quite long but the following highlights are perhaps most relevant for the Church at local and, for that matter, diocesan level: 'Larger than life celebrity leaders who ride in from the outside are negatively correlated with taking a company from good to great.'[2] Also, paying people more is irrelevant, as is distinguishing good from great companies, and so, he believes, is strategy. While there are plenty who believe that Collins is wrong about this, many agree that it's not so much what the strategy is as how it is generated that makes the most difference. Nonetheless Collins insists that great companies don't worry much about what they do – they simply eliminate the things that aren't worth doing. Mergers and technology don't seem to make much difference in determining greatness, nor do launch events, names or tag-lines. Companies do not become great because they just happen to be in the right place at the right time. Moreover, 'the good to great companies paid scant attention to managing change, motivating

---

[1] Collins, J., *Good to Great.* HarperCollins, New York, 2001, p. 21.
[2] Collins, *Good to Great*, p. 10.

people, or creating alignment. Under the right conditions the problems of commitment, alignment, motivation and change largely melt away.'[3]

Plenty of food for thought there! And if I could flag up one particular and paradoxical thing it would be this: the emphasis not on deciding what to do but on deciding what *not* to do. One of the most significant and important practices that I suggest in my book *Beyond Busyness: Time Wisdom for Ministry* is to work not on the to-do list but the *to-don't* list.[4] I have no hard empirical evidence to back this up, but I have a hunch that many clergy could be far more effective in ministry (and therefore be better leaders) if they did less, and tried a little less hard. To spell this out involves uttering the ultimate heresy of contemporary English Anglicanism and to suggest that Bill Vanstone was wrong. Vanstone's Christ on the cross is *not* the model for ordained ministry. It's *not* all about *Love's Endeavour, Love's Expense*. It's all about something much more mundane, less romantic and more participatory and, to be honest, fun. And while I am at it, let me name another heresy: it's okay to disappoint people. Not only okay, but necessary and inevitable. The smart thing is to disappoint with care and attention and good grace. Now that's leadership! To be self-important, and to be relentlessly busy is a sure sign that you are, is something else altogether, even when understood sacrificially.[5]

And the third point is Collins' definition of Level Five leadership, because, strange as it might seem, he hasn't destroyed the concept of leadership but discovered something close to the true heart of it, something deeper than the glossy surface of all-too-many of the success-method books that so beguile and attract us by keying into our fantasies of a lovely pristine new era unfolding under our own squeaky clean and hugely impressive leadership.

---

[3] Collins, *Good to Great*, p. 11.
[4] Cherry, S., *Beyond Busyness: Time Wisdom for Ministry*. Sacristy Press, Durham, 2012, p. 62.
[5] Cherry, *Beyond Busyness*, pp. 99–101.

Anyway, this is it: Level Five leaders have a paradoxical blend of personal humility and professional will. There, the word has slipped out – 'humility' – not humility in a grovelling or weak way, of course, but humility combined with a passion and determination on behalf of their company. It's not, Collins insists, that these leaders lack ego or self-interest, 'they are incredibly ambitious – but their ambition is first and foremost for the institution, not themselves'.[6]

Passionate humility

When I first read about this research I became unduly excited, as it was towards the end of the time when I was writing *Barefoot Disciple: Walking the Way of Passionate Humility*, which I at least intended as a serious contribution, albeit written accessibly with a largely narrative content, to the growing literature on discipleship. This literature (still) lacks, it seems to me, an appropriate questioning of contemporary assumptions about individualism and self-regard, and fails to take into account the huge evidence of mistake-making and relentlessly ongoing learning in the lives of the early disciples of Jesus.

My understanding of discipleship is that it is learning in the company of Christ and Christ's people. Such learning does not encourage us to be complacent or quietist or to accept things as we find them. Rather as disciples we learn to seek first the kingdom of God and to make this our passion. Hence my phrase 'passionate humility' – this is humility with a cause, and passion that has the best possible aspiration and hope, though its feet are firmly and vulnerably on the ground. Such passionate humility, such discipleship is the basis and the school of true leadership.

And this discipleship-based, humble but passionate leadership is not about telling, doing, performing or strategizing, never mind analysing, target setting or monitoring progress. It is a relational

---

[6] Collins, *Good to Great*, p. 21.

and spiritual matter which is not intrinsically difficult but which becomes extremely difficult or even impossible, when people are anxious or narcissistic – two traits that I fear the Church inadvertently encourages in its clergy.

My point here is not that the clergy are reprehensible in their anxiety or their narcissism, rather that it is often the Church that has made them so, and that if the Church wants better leadership (which it almost certainly does, for one reason or another) then it would do well to create an environment that encourages less anxiety and narcissism, because whatever else we are learning about leadership today, it is *not* that anxious narcissists make good leaders. Such people can, of course, be charismatic and popular – indeed this is precisely what they would hope to be – and everyone can shed a tear when they are called to leave their duties for a higher ecclesiastical office, in which their radiant star-likeness can illuminate an even wider territory. But the leadership problem of the Church will not have been eased. Rather it will have been aggravated by preferring the anxious narcissist. As Collins has pointed out, too many senior appointment processes pass over the Level Five leaders in favour of the Level Fours. That's what less than great, anxious organizations do.

Living leadership

Another relevant book from my small library of leadership literature is, like *Good to Great*, based on empirical research. It is called *Living Leadership: A Practical Guide for Ordinary Heroes*. What is brilliant about the research summarized here is that, whereas much leadership work depends on recording what people *say* they do in certain situations, in this case chief executives and others were followed around by researchers who observed them close up and reported on what *actually* happened. Needless to say, what they discovered was a very different story, and one which is much more down to earth and ordinary than the kind of myths about heroic and transformational leadership that even the very good leaders were proffering in their self-reports.

What this research tells us is summarized into three themes by the authors, all of which speak to the leadership dilemmas of the ordained. First, leadership happens *between people* – and it happens *in the moment*. This is an important phrase, suggesting that it is the unplanned, unpremeditated, un-thought-out encounter that makes the most difference. Sometimes people in positional leadership (that's you, vicar/bishop) are seen as heroes, sometimes as scapegoats. That's just the way it is. Don't take it too seriously. Just get along with people as best you can and take small steps forward. You have no idea how much difference for good or ill the odd word or phrase or glance that you didn't notice yourself making will have made.

The second theme is that 'leadership is shaped by context'. That's quite an important bit of jargon to penetrate, because it is code for 'this is not all about me, and so my favoured or default leadership style is a matter of little or no importance'. If you want others to adapt and change to reality, the best thing you can do is adapt and change to reality yourself. This is a theme that is important within yet another good book from my creaking shelf, *Resonant Leadership: Renewing Yourself and Connecting with Others through Mindfulness, Hope and Compassion*, which says that good leadership depends more than anything else on emotional intelligence, and emotional intelligence begins not with self-awareness but with awareness of others. Naturally there is a virtuous dynamic between the two, but church culture has in recent decades colluded with late-modern consumerist values in assuming an essentialist form of individualism that encourages clergy to think that they bring a complete package of gifts and needs into a situation that must accommodate itself to them. At best this is only half the story. The truth is that things go well if accommodation, like listening, is mutual, and based not on role differentiation but respect.

George Binney and his co-authors found that leaders hugely over-estimated the amount of change they could bring to a situation:

'Without exception, the transformations they sought were not achieved.' This doesn't mean that it was all a waste of time and effort, just that 'The results they achieved were more down to earth than the original expectations – though, except in one case, regarded by their companies as successes.'[7]

The third theme emerging from this research is that 'people are most effective when they bring themselves to leading'. This means three things in particular: coming across to others as a real person, not someone who has just read a leadership book (or chapter!) or a 'how to do mission' or 'how to do pastoral care' manual. The chilling insight behind this observation is that people really do know where you are coming from. They can spot fear, or integrity, a mile off because we give ourselves away all the time when we are pretending. They don't say anything, naturally; why should they make themselves vulnerable if you are not already vulnerable with them. They neither trust you nor take any real notice. The second point is connected. True leaders engage their intelligence, emotions and intuitions, and, I would add, their imagination, humour, wit and all their other senses. They come to the 'task' of leadership in the round, as a whole person. And the third point follows completely naturally: such leaders draw on their life experiences.

Conclusions

I no longer feel guilty about reading about leadership, or aspiring to be a better leader. Indeed I have found comfort in discovering a rich vein of work that encourages me to believe that unpopular Christian virtues like humility and diligence are integral to the best leadership, and that the best leaders are (and why should this be a surprise?) on the whole good and positive people who don't necessarily set out to be trusted or to demonstrate their humility

---

[7] Binney, G., Wilke, G. and Williams C., *Living Leadership: A Practical Guide for Ordinary Heroes*. FT Prentice Hall, London, 2009, p. 7.

by acts of public service but who, because of the regard they have for others and their passion for the kingdom of God, and their trust in the superlative and transformative power of grace, have overcome anxiety and the need to prove themselves. We trust great leaders because we can identify with them, not because we admire them – and that means that we need to have leaders, and to be leaders, who are manifestly human, down to earth in their concerns and generous in their attitude to others. I admit that having a vision helps too – but maybe that's the easy bit. Or rather maybe if the vision isn't easy then it is in some way not true, not vocational. 'My burden is easy, my yoke is light,' said the Lord. Somehow that's what needs to be apparent in those who lead. And if the management books and the leadership programmes get us to lighten up for whatever reason, maybe they are worth our time. One thing is clear, a leader who doesn't easily evoke trust is – er, not a leader.

References

Binney, G., Wilke, G. and Williams C., *Living Leadership: A Practical Guide for Ordinary Heroes*. FT Prentice Hall, London, 2009.

Boyatzis, R. and McKee, A., *Resonant Leadership: Renewing Yourself and Connecting with Others through Mindfulness, Hope and Compassion*. Harvard Business School Press, Cambridge MA, 2005.

Cherry, S., *Barefoot Disciple: Walking the Way of Passionate Humility*. Continuum, London, 2011.

Cherry, S., *Beyond Busyness: Time Wisdom for Ministry*. Sacristy Press, Durham, 2012.

Collins, J., *Good to Great*. HarperCollins, New York, 2001.

Covey, S. R., *The Seven Habits of Highly Effective People: Powerful Lessons in Personal Change*. Free Press, New York, 1989.

Greenleaf, R. K., *Servant Leadership*. Paulist Press, New York, 1977.

Vanstone, W. H., *Love's Endeavour, Love's Expense*. Darton, Longman & Todd, London, 1977.

8

Being imaginative

———•◆•———

KATE BRUCE

Will you lead Christ's people in proclaiming his glorious
gospel . . . ? (The Ordinal)

To see a World in a Grain of Sand, And a Heaven in a Wild
Flower. (William Blake)

Imagination matters

Imagination is indispensable in the life of faith. Engaging in prayer,
exploring Scripture, studying new ideas, nurturing learning and
faith in others and communicating effectively all require the engagement of imagination. Imagination is alive in the process of seeing
and naming God in the ordinary, shaping new vision, standing
with the other and reaching out in mission. Arguably threats to
the development of faithful imagination are threats to effective
ministry. Imagination matters.

What do you see?

Picture the scene. It's been a long week. You are tired. You have
half an hour to do the shopping, throw tea together and skim over
the agenda for the evening meeting. With heavy bags, hurrying
hunched into the teeth of a biting wind, all you see is the pavement
passing under your feet.

We all have moments like this when the clamour of the next
pressing demand fills our vision. The problem comes when these

moments feed into an ingrained habit of over-busyness, then insight becomes blurred and imagination atrophies. Superficial seeing is a sure-fire way into superficial teaching and preaching; a ministry that skitters across the surface and fails to reach depth. At the heart of the call to learn, teach and preach lies a question: '*What do you see?*' Really looking and seeing deeply is an imaginative calling into critical reflection that wrestles with the difficult questions of faith. Such an approach to life is not satisfied with how things seem, but seeks a deeper insight beyond the surface, beneath easy platitudes.

The calling to learn, teach and preach, founded on a commitment to pray and grow in wisdom, shapes insight and understanding, affecting how we frame the world and see others and ourselves. This insight cannot emerge in a life full of worthy busyness: there simply isn't space.

The lure of busyness

Busyness is one of the greatest temptations and pitfalls in the complexities of ministerial life. It starts with a siren call. 'All this is so interesting. Who wouldn't want to take on more?' Underneath is an insidious whisper: 'Better work hard. Prove your worth. Please the people.' The irony is that so often the first things to go, to make room for the ever-increasing 'to do' list, are prayer, engagement with Scripture, and theological reading and reflection. These are the very things that underpin effective teaching and preaching. Given that, the discerning 'no' is an important aspect of vocational discernment. '*Do I need to do this? Is there someone better able to do this than me? What will I not do if I accept this commitment?*' Without such discernment clergy find themselves swamped in a mire of expectation which often results in grumpy, tired, resentful ministers who become poor learners and ineffective teachers and preachers. Exhaustion and distraction are obstacles to imagination. With this in mind, ministers need to be encouraged to practise the pause, whether that is the deliberate pause of the scheduled retreat or the regular recollection of the self before God in the midst of a busy day. Related to this need to slow down is the irrevocable connection between the state of the body and our ability to imagine. As embodied beings, if we are tensed up, tired or run down our imaginative insight is distracted and impeded.

Praying the Daily Office, reading and meditating on Scripture, alone and with others, along with prayerful slowing down and attending to God in the everyday shapes our 'on-looks'. An on-look implies greater commitment than an outlook or perspective.[1] On-looks are a way of describing what we 'see', how we look on the world and our part in it. This vision shapes character and feeds back into our praying, learning, teaching and preaching, which in turn have a shaping effect on the community. Part of the task in spiritual formation is to name, encourage and challenge on-looks, our own and those of the church community and wider society. Naming and framing the questions that help to reveal latent on-looks is an imaginative undertaking, which requires noticing attitudes and behaviours which are often habitual and therefore overlooked.

Imagination – theological offside?

It is important to address the potential theological offside flag raised in response to the suggestion that imagination is closely allied to seeing in depth, and is important in all our praying, learning, teaching and preaching. Imagination is sometimes linked to fantasy, deceit and delusion, and might not appear too congenial to the life of faith. The human imagination is vulnerable, often acting from masked self-interest. The fallen nature of humanity means that human imagination is flawed, limited and potentially

---

[1] Evans, D., *The Logic of Self Involvement.* SCM Press, London, 1963, p. 125.

dangerous. Sin can be seen as 'bad imagination',[2] which distorts insight and misconceives the value of the other in relation to the importance of the self. Idolatry is the fruit of 'wrong seeing' or bad imagining. That which is not God, be that power, success, money or influence, is seen as having central importance, and resources are squandered in the pursuit of this imagined ultimate good. The imagination can become folded in upon the self, a source of bitter cogitation and plans of petty vengeance. It can be an agent that leads us to wrong action if we brood on sequences of imagined images of revenge, greed or lust. Undoubtedly, the theological offside flag offers a cautionary note. However, like any other aspect of humanity, imagination can be employed to positive or negative ends.

That imagination can be abused is no reason to oust it from the theological arena. On the contrary when we consider its connection with the reception of revelation it becomes clear that it is vital to faith. However, the vast gulf between God's imagining and the imagination of the human heart apart from God is clear. We need to have the imprint of the divine imagination pressed upon us again and again as we pray individually and corporately and come together to worship and share communion. In relationship with Christ, 'the image of the invisible God' (Colossians 1.15), God judges, reforms and redeems our broken imagining. Imagination shaped by God enables 'right seeing'.

Imagination and revelation

Imagination can be seen as the anthropological point of contact between revelation and human experience.[3] This is not because of any inherent connection it has with God, but simply because it is the point in our experience where revelation is encountered.

---

[2] Green, G., *Imagining God: Theology and the Religious Imagination*. Eerdmans, Grand Rapids MI, 1989, p. 91.

[3] Green, *Imagining God: Theology and the Religious Imagination*. p. 29.

It is the imaginative power (the God-given way in which humans are hardwired) that provides the locus for transcendent revelatory truth to be revealed. Through imagination's gateway, divine truth and human truth intersect.[4]

The content of revelation is an act of grace, but it is received by an ordinary, human capacity, that of imagination. Imagination can be linked to fantasy and deceit, but the point remains that it is also related to truth and discovery. As such it is crucial in the life of prayer, learning, teaching and preaching, and central to mission. Conversion can be seen as new-seeing, a new apprehension of the reality of God found in the muddiness of the ordinary, lifting vision to new heights, redolent with hope and new possibility. The light of such faith dawns in the eye of imagination.

Exploring imaginative function

There are a number of important aspects of the work of imagination. It has a role in our sensory engagement with the world, working with senses stored in memory, combining and re-combining in creative acts, and bringing the sudden intuitive insight that helps us to see in new ways. Imagination has an affective dimension, expressed in our ability to empathize, to feel with another. It also contributes to the formulation of hypothesis and supposition, enabling the construction of argument and underpinning the art of persuasion. In its various functions imagination is important to prayer, reading Holy Scripture, theological learning and communication.

The sensory function of imagination

Rich sensory imagination provides depth to our engagement with the world around us. The startling recognition of the sheer variety

---

[4] Levy, S. M., *Imagination and the Journey of Faith*. Eerdmans, Cambridge, 2008 p. 103.

of colour, taste, sound, smell and texture can lead us more deeply into worship. Openness to the sensory backdrop of natural disaster, famine, war, poverty and suffering can feed into intercession, shaping awareness of the plight of the other and expressing longing for their wholeness.

Sensory imagination is also important for preaching. Ignatius of Loyola encourages an imaginative approach to the biblical text that draws on the sensory and can be an important step in noticing details that might otherwise have been missed, particularly with very familiar passages. With sensory imagination on high alert the preacher can head off on a field trip into the pages of the Bible, foraging for sensory details, throwing them into the knapsack of memory for later consideration.

Reading the Scripture with the sensory imagination raises various questions. What would it mean to walk the landscape of this world? What would be there to see, taste, touch smell, hear? In the cinema screen of imagination the world of the ancient text becomes three-dimensional and can wrap us in its horizons. Such Ignatian exercises reveal where we stand in the text and can contribute to our exegesis and self-understanding. This process offers rich material for preachers to draw on in the sermon creation process as they seek to provoke the imaginative engagement of the hearers, shaping language that is evocative and pictorial.

Sensory imagination is also important as we leave the ancient world behind and in the mind's eye wander through the malls of contemporary culture. What do we see in the headlines? What's the latest on the silver screen? What are the sensory hooks that might speak into the sermon? Are there places where the horizons of the ancient text and the contemporary context fuse? In the pages of Scripture and in the landscape of the present,

> Imagination is like a child roaming the neighbourhood on
> a free afternoon, following first the smell of fresh bread in an
> oven, then the glint of something bright in the grass – led

by curiosity, by hunger, by hope, to explore the world. When imagination comes home and empties its pockets, of course there will be some sorting to do. But do not scold imagination for bringing it all home or for collecting it in the first place.[5]

The intuitive function

Picture a pan on a low heat. Hear the pan lid knocking as the contents simmer; flavours are blending, the temperature rising. What's cooking? The intuitive function is at work. This can't be hurried. Have you ever had the experience of reading a book, or engaging in a conversation, sitting in a class, or writing a sermon when suddenly the penny drops, the lights go on and you see something with greater clarity and depth? You experience the 'aha moment' when now you get it. This is the work of the intuitive imagination coming to the boil. Interestingly, much of the work of the intuitive function takes place beyond our consciousness. Many teachers and preachers will attest to reaching a point in preparation when they find themselves surrounded by scribbled notes and stumped for a way forward. Perhaps after going for a walk, or sleeping on it, the insight comes in a sudden rush, as if from nowhere. The bubbles roil and the pan overflows. Given this, there is wisdom in ensuring that in teaching and sermon preparation time is allowed for the blending and fusing work of the intuitive function or valuable insights may be lost.

In its intuitive function imagination expresses itself in flexibility, in making connections and seeing beyond the obvious, conventional and literal. Intuitive imagination sees patterns and makes links; it transposes, reorders and rearranges material. In this sense, intuitive imagination has a vital function in forming figurative

---

[5] Taylor, B. B., *The Preaching Life*. Cowley Publications, Cambridge MA, 1993, p. 51.

language. It can raise possibilities by combining material to forge new and surprising metaphors, enabling a new 'seeing'.

The intuitive function has a role in shaping sacramental seeing. How does a person apprehend anything of the divine in the ordinary or of the majesty of God transcendent? We can only do this through the grace-filled engagement of the imagination in its intuitive function, which can lift our vision to a perception, albeit 'through a glass darkly',[6] of divinity. In this sense faith must always call upon acts of intuitive imagination, using the material gathered from the world of sensory perception to create figurative forms, pictures that pull back the curtains enabling us to catch a glimpse of transcendent reality. This can feed into prophetic insight that relies on the imaginative vision to perceive alternative vistas of possibility, challenging the dominant narratives of the culture and our collusion with them, offering other ways of being in the world and new horizons of hope.

The affective function

Both sympathy and empathy are aspects of affective imaginative function. We can regard sympathy and empathy as operating on a continuum, with sympathy as 'near-by' affect and empathy as 'inside-affect'. The latter requires a much closer imaginative identi-fication with the situation of the other. Such empathy is epitomized in the advice of Atticus Finch, the lawyer in Harper Lee's novel *To Kill a Mockingbird*, to his daughter: 'You never really understand a person until you consider things from his point of view . . . until you climb into his skin and walk around in it.'[7] It requires that the one trying to understand the feelings of the other imagina-tively projects themselves into their situation. Empathy opens up the potential for vicarious experience, which carries with it

---

[6] 1 Corinthians 13.12.
[7] Lee, H., *To Kill a Mockingbird*. Heinemann, London, 1960, p. 35.

increased knowledge and understanding. We engage the affective imagination when we feel for characters in a novel or film, when we consider their situation as if we were in it ourselves.

When we read the news and project ourselves into the situation of the other the affective imagination is at work. In affective imaginative engagement with biblical characters sympathy can merge into empathy as we shift from imagining, for example Peter's desolation following his denial as if we were Peter in the biblical narrative, to feeling our own guilt and shame connected with the stories of our own denials of Christ. Similarly, we can sympathetically imagine the joy of the younger son, welcomed home in celebration, or we can draw closer and empathetically feel with him the Father's welcoming embrace. Arguably, the affective imagination is the driver for our intercessions as we enter into the plight of the other and stand with them, envisioning hope. Engaging empathetic imagination can generate deep compassion for those who are very different from us, generating the possibility for new insight.

In all teaching and preaching preparation, the affective imagination is profoundly important as we try to inhabit the learner's perspective, asking questions such as: What questions is this idea likely to spark? What are the objections it might generate? How might people feel about this idea or that illustration? How can I communicate in such a way as to captivate engagement? If teaching and preaching is to generate new seeing, it must appeal to people's affective capacities. This is an inherently imaginative undertaking.

The intellectual function

Imagine the scientist hypothesizing, shaping an experiment; the imagination is at work in their 'if . . . then' hypothesizing. This is a reasoned step-by-step process of supposition concerning what might happen and what could be possible. Similarly, structuring a logical reasoned argument means seeing the flow of the discourse, identifying cracks in the argument and taking remedial action. To argue well means anticipating and answering objection, which is an inherently imaginative process. Cicero saw the art of public speech-making being to teach, delight and persuade. Persuasion means helping someone to see the anomalies in their current position and move to a new apprehension. The movement of conversion is itself a paradigm shift, as an old version of reality is set aside and a new one embraced. While conversion might be seen as a matter of affect, it is also a movement of 'if . . . then' logic. Logic, hypothesis and supposition, aspects of the art of persuasion, belong in the toolbox of the intellectual imagination.

One of the interesting aspects of supposition is that we can engage in it without having a commitment to its truth content. We can invite a congregation, in which some may be highly sceptical, to suppose in imagination that the resurrection (for example) occurred and imaginatively explore the possibilities of that supposition even if their current experience is to doubt or deny such a possibility. In such suppositional engagement lies the invitation to faith, which is essentially rooted in the questions '*What if* the gospel accounts of the nature of God are true? Were they to be true, *then what?*' These are fundamentally imaginative questions, with the potential to affect our perception of reality. This argument assumes that there is a connection between our imaginative explorations and the potential effect they have on our apprehension of the external world. What goes on in imagination affects who we are and how we live.

The Church needs ministers whose imaginations are shaped by prayer and Scripture, the image of Christ imprinted deeply in lives that seek to embody the gospel in heart, mind, attitude and behaviour. Shaped by the Spirit, the imaginative minister can have confidence in the power and reality of God present in the muddle of the moment, bringing surprising hope and joy, opening up possibility, engendering new perspective and pulsing with transforming love.

References

Evans, D., *The Logic of Self Involvement*. SCM Press, London, 1963.

Green, G., *Imagining God: Theology and the Religious Imagination*. Eerdmans, Grand Rapids MI, 1989.

Lee, H., *To Kill a Mockingbird*. Heinemann, London, 1960.

Levy, S. M., *Imagination and the Journey of Faith*. Eerdmans, Cambridge, 2008.

Taylor, B. B., *The Preaching Life*. Cowley Publications, Cambridge MA, 1993.

9

Living faithfully

---•—•—

MAGDALEN SMITH

Will you endeavour to fashion your own life and that of your household according to the way of Christ . . . ?

(The Ordinal)

If all hearts were open and all desires known – as they would be if people showed their souls – how many gapings, sighings, clenched fists, knotted brows, broad grins, and red eyes should we see in the market place! (Thomas Hardy)

Removing the mask

It takes courage to take off a mask. Those familiar with the famous story of *The Phantom of the Opera* will recall the mesmerizing moment when Erik lifts his mask to kiss the heroine, Christine, on her forehead. Despite his cruel disfigurement he is astonished to receive a kiss in return. That moment encapsulates how brave we have to be, simply as human people, to show to others the scars and fragilities beneath the surface of who we are. This is felt most keenly by those of us in public life, who bear the continual weight of being responsible and resilient leaders, full of expected *gravitas* and grace. That the boundary between public and private life is diminishing has also become a characteristic of our contemporary age. Programmes such as *The X Factor* demonstrate that what is appropriate to express emotionally in public has changed dramatically over the past few decades.

As a society we remain ever fascinated by the public, private and secret lives of the clergy, with this feeling akin in fascination to other mysterious working worlds, like that of the bookie or the gangster. In television and film, portrayals of clergy (both realistic and parody) abound. Fifty years ago it would have been inconceivable that the inner turmoil and dogged determination necessary for the clerical life might be aired for public viewing in programmes such as *Rev* or *Grantchester*, albeit comically. Based on the novels by James Runcie, *Grantchester* has the archetypical young priest, Sidney Chambers, trying his best to serve as the sincere and loving shepherd to his flock of parishioners, while behind the public persona we witness the darkness of impulsive sex and the beginnings of alcoholism. Yet, in spite of his hidden troubles, Sidney is likeable, sincere, personable, unsanctimonious and, above everything else, human.

In her recent book, *The Collar: Reading Christian Ministry in Fiction, Television and Film*, Sue Sorenson comments that the figure of Adam Smallbone in *Rev* is

> a marvellously well-rounded character. His personality is both devout and irreverent, his ministry a simultaneous disaster and miracle. The weaknesses of Smallbone are grimly and hilariously realistic, but his prayers are genuine conversations with God – the likes of which I have never seen on screen before.

A Canadian, she bemoans the fact that the programme is currently unavailable to wider audiences, because, she says, 'the forgiveness that Smallbone requires is the forgiveness he extends. This transaction is too precious to ignore, whether in fiction or in real life.'[1]

Public and private

The dichotomy between public and private spheres forms part of our shared humanity, which is never the sole domain of the

---

[1] Quoted in 'How to read a cleric', *Church Times*, 16 January 2015, pp. 14–15.

clergy. From an early age, this tension becomes an inherent part of who we are, and how we behave, an instinctive yet slowly imprinted way of behaviour, as we learn that there are certain things we do, or say, privately which we should not do or say in public; like the tattoo we have on a part of our body that we do not normally reveal. But, for clergy, the holding of this is particularly intense, with the expectation that our inner lives should bear a transparent soul, where the maliciousness and temptations of the age should simply pass through, resulting in a private life that is consistently squeaky clean.

Living with such tension is age-old. Mary, the mother of Jesus, carried the weight of what must have been an enormous burden of godly and unexpected responsibility. Interestingly, Gabriel, the bringer of her weighty calling, wisely appears to Mary (certainly in Luke's Gospel) in the privacy of her home. It is as though God gives her the chance to absorb the momentousness of the news in a private space, where she can be truly herself. Poor, pregnant and socially insignificant, she deals with her newfound responsibility by sharing it with her cousin Elizabeth, who has found herself in a similar predicament. It is within the presence of others who understand just what 'this life' feels like when it is lived that we can appropriately exude our joy, share our frustrations, and vent our anger.

Creative tension

Our calling as clergy is to hold both the private and the public closely in tension. This is a complex charge, but, when underpinned by a sustained prayer life, can and should develop naturally. Clergy tend to be reflective people, and the nature of the job means that we are constantly delving into our depths. This can result in inevitable, and worryingly frequent, self-judgement. The pressures of not living up to personal and public expectations can have crushing and disastrous consequences. And yet, such continuous reflection might form part of the salvation of our crisis-ridden Church, for by articulating this process we model something powerful about the potential for human change and the divine life within it.

The American pastor Eugene Peterson describes a particular time in his life when he became acutely aware that, due to the effects of public ministry, his inner attitude was insidiously affecting his love for those within his care. What should have been life-giving water had become a putrid pool of ecclesiastical ambition and restlessness. *Under the Unpredictable Plant* is the record of this internal wrestling. Reflecting on the themes of obedience, faithfulness and honesty, within the book of Jonah, the transformation of his approach to his public role provides a powerful description of how clergy retain their own vocational holiness while grappling with the tension between the public and the private. For this we need the power and presence of Christ always. The figure of Zacchaeus (Luke 19) shows someone whose inner life similarly needed some work because of how it was manifesting itself publically. Encountering Christ in a public space became a conversion experience, as Jesus asks to come into the private domain of this tax collector's home. And it is here, because Jesus deigns to enter that sphere of his life (which becomes a metaphor for his soul) that Zacchaeus is inspired to change dramatically how he operates within his public role.

This takes us to the heart of the matter. For Christ was human as well as God. Jesus was deeply aware of his high calling, as we should be. As priests, our ordination vows charge us with being public representatives of the Church and, to many who do not understand much of this, we are still the 'God-people', observed both innocently as well as, at times, covertly. Those who hate religion look for the excuse, through us, of criticizing the institution, and, more worryingly, of knocking the gospel message itself. Graham Tomlin comments that, as priests, we should always be seeking to be more Christ-like, not because this is most effective in terms of leadership but because it serves as a reminder of the One who is really in charge of the Church. He says this: 'Genuinely priestly leaders are always more worried about what people think of Christ than what people think of themselves.'[2]

Being a public figure

Personally, I enjoy being a public figure. A year or so ago I became the temporary Chaplain to the Mayor of Cheshire East County Council. Not used to such a civic role, I found the experience fascinating, as it brought me into contact with a group of high-powered individuals with whom I had previously had no contact whatsoever, and in the constituency of the Chancellor of the Exchequer. Instinctively, I understood the good sense not to express my own political views, or reservations, but to enjoy the interest this particular set took in me, as a female ecclesial leader and part of the 'world of church'. It was good to be able to inject into a mixed culture of faith, agnosticism and atheism a Christian spirituality. Here, kingdom values of justice, integrity and concern for all God's citizens could be promoted with neutrality, yet also with a deeply held faith conviction. How we talk about God is fundamental, and challenged me in the writing of *Steel Angels*.

The revised Guidelines ask clergy to be people reconciled to God in Christ, as those who strive to be instruments of God's peace in both church and world, building on 2 Corinthians 5. So much of clergy ministry is about healing rifts, which appear suddenly, like old wounds and plastered-over cracks, deeply embedded in our congregations and communities. As leaders who can be simultaneously diplomatic as well as definitive, clergy become people who understand that evolution is usually the preferred way, yet sense when revolution is the timely alternative. Big-picture people,

---

[2] Tomlin, G., *The Widening Circle: Priesthood as God's Way of Blessing the World.* SPCK, London, 2014, p. 148.

inspiring others with corporate vision, yet involved in the private minutiae of people's lives.

How accessible is accessible?

The question of accessibility has long been a thorny issue among clergy and their families. It is refreshing to be reminded that the Guidelines ask for clergy to have a 'reasonable level of availability and accessibility to those for whom they have a pastoral care' (9.2). The parish system, with its fluctuating care of souls, ever dependent on the actual size and nature of a specific 'patch', might make such a statement feel hopelessly fuzzy. But this is our charge, and grapple with it we must. And in a society where unconcern and increased flippancy towards unknown others is increasingly the norm, being public leaders called to respond with graciousness to all has inevitable pastoral and missional impact. But there is a shadow side. In a blanket 'consumer culture' we find that others 'just want a piece of us'. Saying 'yes' to weddings (just to get married in a pretty church) is a classic example, and something many clergy struggle with – a distinctively Anglican problem or opportunity. Thankfully, the Guidelines also speak of 'boundaries', and our remit as people trying to be holy is to patrol these with gentleness and courtesy, as much as we possibly can.

Sunday remains the 'shop window' for the Church and for the clergy, in providing an opportunity to offer to the faithful, as well as to those seeking, something of the nature and power of the gospel and the life of Christ. It is a time, moreover, when clergy must show those who have come to worship the face of compassion and professionalism. The reality in my two-clergy household is a major 'unpacking' (sometimes moaning) session after the four or five services we have been involved in. It happens at the end of a busy morning – a form of letting off steam – as well as genuine reflection, in order for us not to implode after the inevitable frustrations and emotions. We need people to talk to honestly, those who understand something of the dynamics of how ministry affects us; folk who will not berate but can empathize.

Home

The rectory or vicarage is often the multi-dimensional melting pot between what is public and what is private. These houses act as a meeting place, a point of enquiry, a sanctuary, a family home and a place to cry, yell, moan, laugh, as well as to hide. Paradoxically, it is also a place where clergy should be able to be utterly and nakedly themselves, while still being vigilantly ever-ready to respond to whatever is on the other side of the front door or phone line. My own home is simultaneously bustling with the sounds of my son practising the drums, a parishioner needing a quiet word, people arriving for a committee meeting, and a handful of teenagers arriving after school. For me the ideal is to model a place of genuine Christian hospitality to all who enter, an interface between church and world. Some more sensitive souls have commentated on the house's calm and prayerful feel as well as its good order – an important factor, ministry being so often chaotic and creative that we need a physically focused domestic environment, at least to some degree. For others, to sense not the antiseptic perfection of a show home, but an inherent stability at the heart of this public and private intersection, communicates something about the health of the priestly soul, the joy of life and, with this, the nature of God.

The First Letter of Paul to Timothy 3 speaks of the importance of leaders managing the microcosm of their private households, so that they can model something for the larger forum of the community of faith. In the 2013 study *Managing Clergy Lives*, the authors point out that, on the whole, clergy families negotiate the complexities of their lives pragmatically, understanding that living in a vicarage brings both advantages and disadvantages: 'The advent of working spouses, woman priests and two-clergy couples, gay and lesbian clergy relationships and the application of modern employment practices to the clergy have led to a variety of family and household arrangements.'³ They are also cautious in suggesting that vicarage family life is any more demanding than family life elsewhere. Graham Tomlin again:

> If a person is able to build good community life in his or her own family, creating a space where family members are not criticized, domineered or indulged, but nurtured and protected, a place where they can find encouragement, where they can manage their disagreements well and without rancour, where they can return again and again, then that is quite a good indication that that person might be good at leading a church.⁴

Healthy clergy households, which enable those within them to flourish, act as a model for others who are looking for inspiration – homes with Christ at their centre while simultaneously juggling the complexities and brokenness of life.

Tending the household

All clergy need to take seriously their God-given vocations to both marriage and parenting, if these are part of their identity. In the case of same-sex partnerships, this should also be the norm. In *Managing Clergy Lives* it is observed that there are sadly many clergy who sacrifice the sustenance such vocations provide on the pyre of their clerical ministry, stuck in an understanding that a priestly vocation is ultimately more important than putting energy into a healthy and loving partnership. I have found that it is still an anxiety among younger women entering ministry, who come with the practical question of 'How do I balance my vocational priestly calling with bringing up a family?' Thankfully,

---

³ Peyton, N. and Gatrell, C., *Managing Clergy Lives*. Bloomsbury, London, 2013, p. 137.
⁴ Tomlin, *The Widening Circle*, p. 150.

20 years into ordained female leadership there are women who can offer a more holistic and reassuring model of how to interweave these callings. The importance of boundaries is crucial (both my husband and I grew up with clergy fathers who would get up to answer a ringing phone during mealtimes), as is respect for the professional life of the spouse, and an awareness of how the well-being and happiness of personal relationships and families can grow and be sustained. Part of good modelling is not to compartmentalize our clerical 'tasks' compared with the rest of our lives – the two interconnect. A classic example is the school-gate ministry, and the pastoral conversations that happen naturally, as we wait for our own children to finish their school day. Another might be how clergy organize their own finances using ethical choices, careful stewardship for the future as well as practising generosity to church and charity, modelling an attitude of gratitude in how we interpret and accept the gifts that are given to us daily.

Yet clergy do need times when they can metaphorically 'take the collar off', by having a decent amount of time for family holidays, days out with spouse, or good friends if we are single. Occasions when we are seen to relish the good things in life – food, hobbies, art and the natural world – not only give those in our charge permission to do the same, but model something powerful about how God is deeply embedded in the gift which is our life. Taking care of our physical well-being, by taking time to exercise regularly, communicates that we are stewards for our bodies, which are indeed temples of God's Spirit, to be nurtured and cared for. Most clergy know from painful experience that there is nothing heroic about overwork, although there are times when we go beyond tiredness as an inevitable part of a vocation that is rightly costly. Working in a job that is 'leggy' and intangible often breeds stress as we reflect at the end of a difficult week, 'What have I actually achieved?', forgetting that it is never our own achievements but our accompanying the work of the Holy Spirit. There is something here about good order in terms of our own spiritual life – the cultivation of an ascetic discipline of a rock-solid inner reliance on the living God, to whom we return daily. I have noticed over the last few years that I pray best at home rather than in church, for church is the place where I am publically on show as professional Christian. What matters is that through the privacy of time alone with God, however it is done, we rediscover an exquisite tenderness and profound acceptance of ourselves, which spills over into our role as confident yet humble leaders of public worship.

Conclusion

As clergy, our language is particularly relevant, for we cannot fulfil our professional role without using our voices. Within Galatians 5.22–23, the fruit of the Spirit includes self-control. Although the walls in our rectory have absorbed some inevitable verbal diatribes over the years, I must admit to an intense dislike of hearing clergy swear in any kind of public forum. As we attempt to model holiness, the impact of bad language feels not only ugly but strangely unnecessary – for people whose words are meant to be prophetically distinctive, by the nature of their wisdom, balm, joyful hope and rightful challenge. Surely, we can be more than distinctive as clergy if we use speech gently, beautifully and with appropriate cogency, in society's millpond, where speech is often barked, unarticulated and verbose.

J. K. Rowling's novel *The Casual Vacancy*, serialized on BBC1 in 2014, brilliantly demonstrates the challenge of preventing private angst spilling over into the public domain. Set in the fictional and quintessential West Country town of Pagford, the novel describes the race to fill the 'casual vacancy' of a seat on the local parish council. Those running for the position soon find their despicable secrets revealed on the Council's online forum, ruining their personal reputations and election campaigns. The fact that the novel was the fastest-selling book in the United Kingdom in three years of its publication perhaps demonstrates our society's insatiable fascination with the interface between the public and the private, as variations of this age-old theme are continuously played out in the arts and media.

For clergy, when the public domain is so often willing to soak up our own darknesses as a sheet of blotting paper does with ink, this challenge is particularly steep. To avoid soul-wreckage we need to accept, and relish, a lifelong balanced humanity and vocation that is vulnerably holy; one that seeks to establish a transparent private life and spirituality that can be genuinely practised in the public domain also. This ongoing dynamic should enable us to establish right boundaries, so that we remain grounded, while being shrouded with something of the holiness and humanity of Jesus: a lifelong love affair that sustains, guides and heals.

References

Hardy, T., 'Diary entry 18 August 1908', in Hardy, F. E., *The Later Years of Thomas Hardy*. Macmillan, London, 1930, p. 133.

Peterson, E., *Under the Unpredictable Plant: An Exploration in Vocational Holiness*. Eerdmans, Grand Rapids MI, 1992.

Peyton, N. and Gatrell, C., *Managing Clergy Lives*. Bloomsbury, London, 2013.

Rowling, J. K., *The Casual Vacancy*. Little, Brown and Company, London, 2012.

Runcie, J., *Sidney Chambers and the Shadow of Death: Grantchester Mysteries Book 1*. Bloomsbury, London, 2012.

Smith, M., *Steel Angels: The Personal Qualities of a Priest*. SPCK, London, 2014.

Sorenson S., *The Collar: Reading Christian Ministry in Fiction, Television and Film*. Cascade Books, Eugene OR, 2014.

Tomlin, G., *The Widening Circle: Priesthood as God's Way of Blessing the World*. SPCK, London, 2014.

10

Keeping well

————◆◆◆————

DAVID WALKER

You cannot bear the weight of this calling in your own strength.   (The Ordinal)

He had resided in Italy for twelve years. His first going there had been attributed to a sore throat; and that sore throat, though never repeated in any violent manner, had stood him in such stead, that it had enabled him to live in easy idleness ever since.   (Anthony Trollope[1])

In the psychiatrist's chair

At the age of 42, ordained over 16 years and team rector of a growing and lively benefice, I went into therapy. For the next 12 months I spent an hour each week in conversation with a Jungian analyst who was a member of the diocesan counselling team. My principal motivation was that my wife, studying for a counselling diploma, was already benefiting from a similar engagement. It took only a session or two for me to begin to feel that I was at last getting to grips with some of what lay at the core of my being, things that for the rest of the time got pushed to one side by the continuous demands of both professional and personal life. I became a better person, a better Christian and a better vicar. And the understanding that this was the aim was what avoided it

---

[1] Anthony Trollope, introducing the Reverend Dr Vesey Stanhope in *Barchester Towers*. Longmans, London, 1857.

becoming self-indulgent. Part way through the year I learned that I was to be ordained bishop, but would have to keep the fact a secret for almost three months. My weekly session, sitting in a chair not lying on a couch, kept me rather more level-headed than would otherwise have been possible.

The story of my therapy is one that I can tell easily, because I've told it often. I learned to tell it in order to help others, especially fellow clergy, feel that accessing help and support, whatever the motivation, is not a sign of weakness or failure, but of a commitment to our personal well-being. Well-being is not, primarily, about how we respond to dysfunctionality; it's about functioning more effectively. It's not about eradicating some abnormality; it's about doing normal, and doing it well.

Understanding well-being

Spiritual before practical

The section of the Guidelines that relates to well-being begins, like the other sections, with a short quotation from the Ordinal. Well-being is God's gift to us, and is mediated, above all else, through Scripture and Spirit. The habit of immersing ourselves daily in the former and being ever ready to receive from the latter represents the priority of the divine dimension in transforming us from what we have been to what, by God's grace, we shall become. The centrality of the disciplined rhythm of prayer to the life of clergy has been covered earlier in this book; a brief reminder here will help us avoid the trap of seeing well-being as a purely human construct, to be attained by human effort.

Broken open is not broken down

The goal that 'all shall be well' is as much eschatological for us as individuals as it is for the creation, which Julian of Norwich saw in her vision. So it is to that that the Guidelines refer, the 'broken humanity' from which we minister.

One of the key moments during my time at theological college was the discovery that God had not just called me because of my gifts and strengths, nor had he called me *despite* my imperfections. His call was to me in my entirety. It would be as much through my weaknesses as through my strengths that I would be serving him as a priest. The concept of 'appropriate vulnerability' has become an increasingly important one to me. The very wounds that we bear from our journey thus far enable us to minister to others whose situations reflect something of what we have been through (or may still be experiencing) ourselves. When we expose those wounds not only is it unsurprising that they sometimes hurt and bleed again but it is right that, to an extent, they do. Those who are called to the most regular and intensive pastoral work will almost certainly benefit from having supervision in the form common in the counselling world. For other clergy, there will be value in participating in such supervision for a limited period, while engaged in a particular pastoral relationship and task. Increasingly, group supervision provides a more collegial, and more economical, alternative to individual.

Different is not bad

Many clergy will have taken part in a Belbin test, made use of the enneagram or know their Myers Briggs type. All of these instruments afford an understanding of the ways in which we are psychologically different and therefore how we will operate differently from others, take up distinctive roles in a team situation and even have distinct preferences for how we pray. The development of a 'Theology of Individual Differences' by Leslie Francis and others,[2] sets a framework in which we can articulate more clearly that neither the love of God nor the mission of the Church are preferentially directed towards some types more than others.

---

[2] Leslie Francis is Director, Warwick Religions and Education Research Unit.

The practical tools listed in the previous paragraph enable us to identify our preferred ways of operating. Further, they help us to understand why we find certain types of engagement, and some people, more difficult and stressful to engage with than others. To know that I am different from the majority of my fellow clergy, and therefore that my call is not to mimic their patterns and methods, can bring a great sense of release.

One response is to narrow the scope of our mission, focusing as much as possible on the tasks and people congenial to our own type. Realistically, however, the sheer range of roles and responsibilities that go with ordained ministry make this as unlikely in practice as it is unsound in theology. A better strategy is to work with the insights that one or more of these psychological tools provide and to balance our working time (as well as our leisure) so that there are enough things that re-energize us and enhance our sense of engagement to compensate for the things that drain and deplete us. As ordained ministry becomes increasingly collaborative it becomes ever more important for our well-being to know how we fit into, and offer our best through, both formal and informal teams.

Satisfied or exhausted?

Over recent years a number of studies have sought to explore the notion of 'burnout' among clergy. The factors that contribute to this are many and varied. Some are direct consequences of particularly conflicted or dysfunctional situations in the parish or ministry context. Others are significantly impacted by patterns in our own behaviour: not taking holidays and days off; unwillingness to say 'no' to requests; an unhealthy understanding of self-sacrifice; not attending to a proper work–life balance. Burnout is not irrecoverable; it lies within but at the end of the scale of normal experience.

The more extreme symptoms of clergy stress are the same as with other professions, among them: alcohol dependency; use of illegal or prescribed drugs; domestic abuse; aberrant sexual behaviour; uncontrolled personal debt; misappropriation of funds. Such behaviours are unlikely to ameliorate while the underlying stress remains unaddressed. Early intervention is always better than leaving it for later. Look out for any changes in your own pattern of behaviour and seek help either through your diocese or your doctor. Listen to what your closest family and friends are saying about changes they have perceived in you.

More recently, research has uncovered that many clergy thrive notwithstanding that they report factors indicative of high levels of exhaustion. In 2014 clergy topped an Office of National Statistics scale for job satisfaction report,[3] while public house landlords, who face a similarly complex task of handling premises, people and finance in a local community context, came bottom. The adoption of 'balanced' models of clergy stress, which include scales for satisfaction as well as exhaustion, suggest that the high sense of fulfilment that many clergy receive through their ministry serves as an effective bulwark against burnout. In practice this means that ensuring a sufficient proportion of time is spent engaged in those tasks and roles that provide the most satisfaction may be as effective, and certainly more achievable, than relying entirely on seeking to reduce the exhaustion factors. It also provides a warning that your well-being may be seriously at risk not because the exhaustion levels have gone up but because something has happened that reduces your satisfaction.

Can I help you?

After God, the Guidelines repeatedly emphasize the importance of other people. Clergy are called to be those who 'receive ministry' as well as provide it to others. Dioceses have a number of people and facilities in place which seek to assist clergy in managing their

---

[3] <www.bbc.co.uk/news/magazine-26671221>

own well-being. Other forms of support are accessible through individual negotiation. Crucially, these are not remedial actions required by bishops in order to correct failings or to deal with capability concerns. Their concern is with the normal, not the abnormal or aberrant. This section explores some of the methods currently accessed by clergy for support, with the exception of spiritual direction, which has been covered in an earlier chapter.

Reasonable costs associated with accessing support should be reimbursed through the local PCC or other expenses provider. If all else fails by way of covering costs, speak with your archdeacon who may have access to discretionary or other clergy charitable funds.

Ministerial development review

The various local forms of review set up by most dioceses by the late 1990s were formalized into the current concept of ministerial development review (MDR), which, as the Guidelines point out, is a legal obligation for ordained ministers holding common tenure and a matter of good practice for other licensed clergy. Individual dioceses retain freedom to set up schemes in the manner the bishop feels most suited to their needs, subject to compliance with national guidelines. MDR meetings take place at least once every two years and seek to identify a small number of key priorities for the period to the next review, along with any training and development needs. As well as helping an individual minister to reflect on the recent past and identify manageable aims for the future, these meetings enable the bishop and his or her staff to gain a sense of where there are similar issues being repeatedly identified and that merit a larger-scale response. Most clergy find MDR to be affirming. Some balk at the several hours typically necessary to complete the preparatory paperwork; however, the self-reflection this facilitates can be the most productive element of the process. The fact that MDR is 'on the record', and that the review is conducted and seen by those who may be considered to have influence over the future ministerial prospects of the reviewee, can limit the extent to which clergy feel able to discuss difficulties and weaknesses.

Work consultancy and mentoring

While some dioceses have from time to time made specific offers of work consultancy, mentoring or coaching, by and large these support structures for ministry are individually accessed by clergy on their own initiative. A diocese may maintain a list of possible providers. Mentors, who are most often volunteers drawn from the ranks of experienced ministers, typically work with an individual after a significant ministerial change, for example with first incumbents and newly ordained bishops. In wider society, mentoring is used to prepare a person in advance of a move to a more senior role. It has a particular part to play in working with those from groups underrepresented in senior positions, such as women and candidates from minority ethnic backgrounds who benefit from preparation for the additional challenges they will face. Mentors may be drawn from outside the Church.

Work consultancy operates in a similar manner to mentoring except that it is less focused on periods of transition and may have, by comparison, a greater emphasis on the work tasks than on the development of the individual. In consequence meetings with a work consultant may be less frequent, perhaps only annually, than would be expected from a mentoring arrangement. Both work consultancy and mentoring are often delivered by individuals working in the same field as the recipient. They are also quite commonly free of charge, being seen primarily as passing on wisdom and insight to the next generation.

Coaching and action learning sets

Recent years have seen considerable growth in the use of one-to-one coaching across a range of professional sectors in the UK. This rapid growth, together with the unregulated nature of the work, has led to some variability of quality. Full-time professional coaches offer their services across a wide range of sectors and the costs of engaging one with a strong track record can be significant. Where coaching has been established for some time there is a strong evidential base for its effectiveness in improving work outcomes, and hence would be likely to improve well-being. At its best, coaching is non-directive and allows an individual to focus on a small number of specific issues being faced at work. It is focused less on practical 'tips for the trade' than mentoring and work consultancy, as the provider is not an expert in the recipient's field. However, it allows exploration of the feelings, mental attitudes, past experiences, habits and fears that inhibit both work effectiveness and well-being. Coaching is often undertaken for a fixed period of time, typically a year or two. Some dioceses are beginning to explore making coaching available free to clergy.

Action learning sets are a development of the coaching model, where typically three or four individuals working separately but in the same field meet together on a regular (perhaps quarterly) basis with a coach/facilitator. The peer element allows a deeper level of understanding of the particular demands and challenges of the work of the participants, while the facilitator provides the coaching techniques. The costs of the coaching are shared but the time element is increased. Working alongside colleagues allows every participant to be supporting every other, which itself can provide a boost to self-worth and well-being.

Continuing ministerial education (CME)

CME is a catch-all term for a very wide range of services that can add to well-being. Most dioceses will have a programme of CME days or sessions to which all licensed clergy are invited, and which may be a requirement for those on common tenure. Alongside this, many clergy will have access to a small diocesan grant each year, typically around 1 per cent of stipend, to which they can apply to pay for events run by outside bodies. Larger grants may be available for those undertaking formal studies leading to higher qualifications such as master's degrees and professional or academic doctorates. The *Experiences of Ministry* survey,[4] carried out in conjunction with King's College, London, suggests that engaging in study that is related to an individual's ministerial context has a positive impact on levels of engagement. CME should help us to develop the skills of reflection on our ministerial practice, to look at a problem or issue from other perspectives, and to offload some of our fears and concerns through informal conversation with supportive peers. The coffee breaks can be as important as the content!

Counselling and therapy

Counselling and psychotherapy can be accessed through the National Health Service via the patient's GP. However, the cost of the services to the NHS and the waiting times required mean that such provision will tend to focus on the most high-level cases, where mental health is significantly depleted. Counselling as a tool for well-being is more likely to be accessed through the diocese. Such services are normally available to all licensed clergy, and in many cases are extended to cover the immediate household members of ministers. The offer can be variable across the country as to the number of sessions, the extent to which the costs of the service are borne by diocese and by participant, and whether it is provided purely in cases where the recipient is under significant stress or more widely. While the service is commissioned by the diocese, the details of who has accessed it, the content of sessions and any outcomes are confidential to the counsellor and client. A bishop may not request a report from the counsellor to demonstrate that an individual has accessed the service or has satisfactorily 'dealt with' some problem.

---

[4] <www.kcl.ac.uk/sspp/departments/management/research/experiencesofministry.aspx>

Being a good diocese

The bulk of this chapter has focused on how an individual member of the clergy can identify issues of well-being and access services that may help to improve it. As office holders, the primary responsibility for well-being lies with the individual minister, not with an employer. The previous section has listed the primary areas of support that dioceses typically provide and that clergy can access both individually and collegially. However, a diocese that takes well-being to heart will want to go some way beyond such services, and identify with clergy those aids for and impediments to well-being that go beyond specific individual cases. The culture of a diocese can also have some bearing on clergy well-being in terms of feeling valued and cared for, understanding where they fit into the life of the diocese and how their particular ministries contribute to its overall mission and purpose.

The Manchester clergy well-being survey covers a range of topics, from parsonage housing via fundraising to the frequency and impact of callers to the vicarage who are perceived to have mental health problems. It identifies areas in which clergy are broadly satisfied and fulfilled in their work and those that cause them worry, fear or concern. The information is collected anonymously via an internet questionnaire facility. Undertaking such a survey allows a diocese to identify areas of its own work where some change or reconfiguration can reduce problems. Repeating a survey on a regular basis, perhaps every few years, allows emerging trends to be uncovered and addressed. The data can be segmented in order to look at well-being issues that affect particular groups of clergy, such as self-supporting ministers and those who serve in parishes in the top 10 per cent of deprivation levels.

Conclusion

This chapter has sought to make the case for understanding clergy well-being and for engaging in a range of individual, group and diocesan activities that support it. The danger is that all this can feel like yet more things to crowd into a packed diary and yet more costs to be absorbed by a system that ultimately relies on voluntary parish contributions. Against such concerns it will need to be repeatedly stressed that poor well-being is costly, first in human terms and then in the time and money spent in seeking to remedy a bad situation. It impairs both the individual and the community in responding to God's call.

Conversely, and bluntly, good attention to well-being makes the mission of the Church both more effective and easier to afford.

References

King's College, London, *The Experiences of Ministry Survey*. <www.kcl.ac.uk/ sspp/departments/management/research/experiencesofministry.aspx> Trollope, A., *Barchester Towers*. Longmans, London, 1857.

Part 3

THE FUTURE

11

Trusting clergy

ROBERT INNES

In the name of our Lord we bid you remember the greatness
of the trust that is now to be committed to your charge.

(The Ordinal)

How can we increase trust? By being more trustworthy.

(Timothy Jenkins[1])

Trust and suspicion

There is much debate about what to call the complex age in
which we live. It goes under various guises – 'late capitalism',
'late modernity', 'postmodernity'. It is as much about feelings
as facts, and can take us in fanciful directions if we let it. It is a
period characterized by an emphasis on the individual and his
or her pleasures and needs. Identity is increasingly conferred
through an acquired 'lifestyle'. This is not such recent a phenomenon either. Writing nearly 70 years ago about W. B. Yeats,
Auden noted that Yeats was faced with what he called the 'modern
problem', namely that of living in 'a society no longer supported
by tradition without being aware of it', where individuals wishing
to bring order and coherence into their sensations, emotions
and ideas are forced to do deliberately for themselves what

---

[1] Quoted in Harrison, J., Innes, R. and van Zwanenberg, T., *Rebuilding Trust in Healthcare*.
Radcliffe Medical Press, Abingdon, 2003, p. 173.

'in previous ages had been done by family, custom, church, and state'.[2]

Rowan Williams, in his book *Lost Icons*,[3] laments that we are becoming unable to picture ourselves other than through the language of consumer choice. In such a world, other people, even our children, are seen as 'competitors'. Fellowship, charity and trust become ever more difficult to realize. Moreover, society begins to shape its members first and foremost as those who must learn to play the consumer role, with 'me' at the centre. With that comes a loss of 'social capital', something the American sociologist Robert Putnam notes has halved in the USA in the space of four generations.[4]

But have we become less trusting in the process? Not according to Onora O'Neil in her 2002 Reith Lectures.[5] She cast doubt on polls and newspapers that gleefully report declining public trust. For her, our actions suggest a continuing willingness to place trust in others – family members, neighbours, friends, as well as members of professions and public institutions, even the ones we profess not to trust! It would seem that actions do speak louder than words.[6]

O'Neil is clear that we do not live in a culture of 'mistrust' – usually, individuals do not refuse to place their trust in banks, businesses, hospitals and churches. Equally, she is clear that we do live in a culture of 'suspicion', where professionals and institutions are expected to demonstrate clearly and convincingly why others

---

[2] Auden, W. H., 'Yeats as an Example', *Kenyon Review*. Kenyon College, Gambier OH, Spring 1948, pp. 191–2.

[3] Williams, R., *Lost Icons*. Continuum, London, 2000, pp. 22–4.

[4] Putnam, R., 'Bowling alone: America's declining social capital', *Journal of Democracy*. National Endowment for Democracy, Washington DC, January 1995, http://muse.jhu. edu/login?auth=0&type=summary&url=/journals/journal_of_democracy/ v006/6.1putnam.html

[5] O'Neil, O., *A Question of Trust: The BBC Reith Lectures 2002*. Cambridge University Press, Cambridge, 2002.

[6] A view supported by a National Centre of Social Research study reported in *The Times*, 14 May 2015, p. 19.

should continue to trust them – hence the proliferation of guidelines and protocols. But we must note that suspicious cultures may perversely generate activities that make the problem worse – espousing individual rights without corresponding duties; breeding target-driven, bureaucratic modes of 'accountability'; encouraging types of 'transparency' that fail to expose deceit; and fuelling a toxic and suspicious media culture. But this is where we are, and how to develop a more trusting culture is our task.

A view from theology

Those brought up in the world of theology know 'trust' and 'faith' to be of central importance. Indeed, throughout the Bible, the relationship between God and humankind is described principally through the category of faith. This faith involves holding together three elements: knowledge of what to believe (*notitia*), intellectual acceptance of its truth (*assensus*) and a personal commitment to that truth (*fiducia*). And Scripture doesn't so much encourage 'blind faith' but promotes 'questioning faith'.[7]

As we journey with the lectionary through certain Old Testament books – Job, Psalms and Ecclesiastes come to mind – it seems that serious questioning of faith in the face of suffering and meaninglessness is quite legitimate. It is as if no agenda item is inadmissible. Here the opposite of faith is not so much questioning and doubt as cynicism and rebellion. It is the failure to trust a trustworthy God that is seen as a sign of human weakness and error.

But is faith (or trust) a divine gift? Or is it a human decision? The answer to this may well depend on how Catholic we are – faith as an 'active' quality flowing from human understanding and personal decision-making; or how Protestant – where faith is a 'passive' quality given by divine grace. The same issue can arise in human relationships, where trust might be thought to be the

---

[7] Harrison, Innes and van Zwanenberg, *Rebuilding Trust in Healthcare*, p. 17.

decision of the one who trusts, rather than a response to qualities emanating from the one to be trusted.

From the earliest times, the evidence from Scripture is of families and peoples building communal lives founded on trust. Whether in the covenants with Abraham, or through the law given to Moses, a legal and moral system developed which exalted trustworthiness and denounced falsity and corruption. Equally, the first Christian communities based their life together on a 'new covenant' – one that embodied a love that 'bears all things, believes all things, hopes all things, endures all things' (1 Corinthians 13.7). Some versions replace the words translated as 'believes all things' as 'always trusts'. The call to trust and to believe became inseparable.

Yet while God can truly be trusted, there is suspicion in the Scriptures about how much human beings should be trusted, notably those with political power. With few exceptions, Old Testament kings are presented as untrustworthy; even the heroes of the faith demand caution in the area of their trustworthiness – Jacob and his dealings with Esau; Joseph, his brothers and the deception of the silver cup; and David, Bathsheba and the murder of Uriah come to mind.

A view from sociology

There is reasonable caution in looking beyond theology and philosophy for answers to deep questions of belief and meaning. Yet other academic disciplines, such as anthropology, psychology and sociology can and do offer valid and illuminating insights into complex issues.

Writers such as Francis Fukuyama,[8] Barbara Misztal[9] and Anthony Giddens[10] have explored the nature of social trust and

---

[8] Fukuyama, F., *Trust: The Social Virtues and the Creation of Prosperity*. The Free Press, New York, 1995.

[9] Misztal, B., *Trust in Modern Societies*. Basil Blackwell, Oxford, 1996.

[10] Giddens, A., *The Third Way*. Polity Press, Cambridge, 1998, pp. 78–86.

how it influences economies and the way in which we are governed; of how the idea of civic society has an impact on questions of mutual accountability and trust. The sociologist Piotr Sztompka[11] offers a particularly fascinating study. Although his focus is on the absence of trust in his native Poland, followed by attempts to rebuild trust after the fall of communism, his analysis resonates not just in political contexts but in, for example, those of medicine and the Church.

Sztompka analyses trust in four ways ('foundations') – primary trust, secondary trust, the trusting impulse and the trust culture. His understanding covers similar ground to the theological model of *notitia, assensus* and *fiducia* mentioned above, although for Sztompka trust is a thoroughly 'active' quality to be distinguished from the more passive commodity of what he calls 'confidence'. The decision to trust is a rational one, made after weighing up the odds. Stzompka makes bets about the future actions of others, and remains responsible for his own actions, no longer blaming others, the regime or the system if and when something goes wrong.[12]

So how are we to understand his various types of trust – personal (primary), institutional (secondary) and psycho-social (the trusting impulse and cultures of trust)? Simply put, in a church context, I might say that I trust the vicar (primary – from my good experience of messy church), but not the diocese (secondary – they built houses on our nice glebe field); I tend to trust others, as I grew up in a very caring, supportive family (trusting impulse – positive propensity to trust others) but the village feels quite angry and cynical about issues (trust culture – negative, militating against trust). How this model helps an understanding of trust in the Church more widely will be discussed later in the chapter.

---

[11] Sztompka, P., *Trust: A Sociological Theory*. Cambridge University Press, Cambridge, 1999.
[12] Sztompka, *Trust*, p. 25.

Trust and discipline

If section 12 of the Guidelines is devoted to the theme of 'trust', then it should be noted that it is preceded by section 11 on 'discipline'. For our purposes it has been important to start with trust and then to move on to discipline, for as section 12.1 notes 'The development of trust is of primary importance for honest relationships within ministry.' The next sub-sections speak of how clergy exert positions of power and authority over others, ranging from other clergy and ministers, lay church members, and the parish as a whole. The issues of safeguarding, the abuse of power and of maintaining proper relational boundaries are discussed, with advice on matters of consent and confidentiality given.

New methods of communication and the use of social media need careful handling. The ability to send emails instantaneously, and to multiple recipients, can lead to complications. How much to reveal of oneself – one's inner thoughts and feelings? The temptation to react without taking time to reflect may lead to misunderstandings and hurt. During my ministry in Brussels, we introduced an 'email policy' as a way of trying to bring a godly etiquette to the way in which we interacted through new media.

The Guidelines warn against bullying and the misuse of power, which can work in many different directions – clergy on clergy, laity on clergy, clergy on laity, laity on laity. And bullying is that which is perceived and experienced by the one being bullied, even if that is not the explicit intention of the one who bullies. It is all too easy to manipulate, to pressurize or to seek to control or to denigrate another person or persons. There is the need for each of us to be watchful and to be ready to intervene in appropriate ways where we suspect such action for it is 'all our business'.

The place of discipline in this context is to step in when trust has been broken and others exploited or let down. It is the necessary counterbalance to trust, although it cannot of itself rebuild trust.

The Guideline on discipline

Section 11 on 'discipline' covers how clergy work with others in building God's kingdom. This activity is undergirded by patterns of relationships shaped and ordered by legal documents and a range of commitments. In particular, the *Canons of the Church of England*[13] are singled out for comment, as well as a pointer to the regulations made by the bishop of the diocese concerned.

Mention is made of the Clergy Discipline Measure, originally formulated in 2003 and amended in 2013 and 2015.[14] The Measure has the important formal role of providing a mechanism to test out breaches of trust, malpractice and misconduct. It is not the instrument to deal with questions of doctrinal concern, nor of poor performance related to ill-health or incompetence. There is no doubt that its presence creates anxiety among clergy, and that is not unreasonable. The implementation of the Measure is monitored by the Clergy Discipline Commission,[15] where both the Chair and Deputy Chair have notable experience at the highest level within the English judicial system. An annual report is produced and the Commission seeks to be transparent in its dealings as much as confidentiality and due process allow.

Caring for the carers

The final section of the Guidelines, section 14, concerns itself with 'care for the carers'. Part of that care is the responsibility to protect all clergy, but particularly those newly ordained, from the abuses

---

[13] Church of England, *Canons of the Church of England*, 7th edn, <www.churchofengland. org/about-us/structure/churchlawlegis/canons/canons-7th-edition.aspx>

[14] Church of England, *Clergy Discipline Measure*, https://www.churchofengland.org/media/ 2192477/cdm%202003%20amended%20by%20cd%28a%29m%20as%20published%20 feb%202014.pdf

[15] The Clergy Discipline Commission has a membership of 12; my co-editor Jamie Harrison is currently an appointed member, <www.churchofengland.org/about-us/structure/ churchlawlegis/clergydiscipline/cdc.aspx>

of power already discussed (14.1). Caring for clergy is everyone's responsibility, not least that of the laity in partnership with the diocese. The bishop has a particular role, sharing his or her responsibility with other key members of the team.

The introduction of common tenure has brought a different set of challenges and expectations. Working in local clergy teams, within benefices or across deaneries, adds to the complexity. Isolation has always been a risk, but it may not necessarily be reduced under these newer arrangements – one can still be on one's own in a 'team'. And again the reality of the possibility of bullying (14.5) is noted.

How trust can be strengthened – primary trust

And so back to Piotr Stzompka and his ideas on how trust 'works' in practice. For Stzompka, *primary trust* relates to what makes a person or institution worthy of trust, namely their traits and qualities. This is of first importance and involves both their reputation and how they perform.

People trust clergy because of the reputation that clergy have as a profession and because of good experiences of individual clergypersons. Those outside the Church are influenced by what they see or hear of clergy at a distance – in the press, both local and national. Stories of clergy misdemeanours have a negative effect on this 'general reputation' (when one suffers all suffer). On the other hand, strong and positive profiles of national church leaders – our archbishops, say, or heroic stories about local clergy, have a correspondingly uplifting effect. For fringe attenders, every contact with the local clergyperson counts. Trust is built slowly on the basis of repeated good experiences.

Within the local church community, a minister's fund of trust is a precious resource which takes time to build. In *Leading with Trust*, Richard England describes well the puzzlement of the new curate who can't see why people won't accept his ideas – until his training vicar gently explains to him that his ability to inspire depends not just on his vision but equally on the trust that people feel in him.[16] Steven Covey's concept of 'the speed of trust' is helpful: a good leader will have a sense of the pace at which change can be implemented and will deploy appropriate patience when trust is still developing and people are correspondingly cautious.

Integrity matters. All that we say or do, particularly in the early days, contributes to or detracts from our stock of trust. Folk notice whether the minister is the same person in the pulpit as in the staff meeting, or in casual conversation. In my first parish, someone suggested that it would be two years before my sermons would be truly 'heard'. That may have been unduly pessimistic, but others needed the assurance that I practised what I preached and didn't preach what I didn't practise. As a teenager, I remember being shocked when I received a lift in the vicar's car. I was horrified by the aggression and bad language with which he responded to other motorists.

Developing high levels of *self-awareness and emotional intelligence* as we deal with others makes for high-trust encounters. *Clarity and consistency* in our speaking conveys honesty and reliability. (This has been a particular challenge for me – in working in international congregations I have come to realize that English understatement and allusiveness is easily read as evasiveness.) *Being good at what we do*. We can't always be perfect but we can strive for excellence. *Loving our people*. It may be a cliché but this way of being is at the heart of the ministerial vocation; people will forgive a lot if they sense that there is genuine concern for them and for their well-being.

Building cultures of trust

Secondary trust concerns itself with the institutional environment, and the systems in which we function. Good systems of clergy

---

[16] England, R., *Leading with Trust*. Grove Books, Cambridge, 2015.

selection, training, appointment, licensing, review and discipline should have the effect of building trust in those who lead. Broadly speaking these systems are attended to with a great deal of care and concern, and they work well. In some areas we could improve – for example, where congregations have proper concerns in the area of 'capability', it is not always easy to deal effectively with clergy who (while not having committed any misdemeanour) are manifestly under-performing. And there will occasionally be mistakes – someone slips through the net who should never have been ordained; a disastrous appointment is made. The thing about mistakes is to learn from them. The conduct of formal 'lessons learned' exercises in the wake of safeguarding cases is an example.

Attending to issues of secondary trust at the local level requires something of a culture change, especially in the area of safeguarding. I well remember the consternation with which the church council of which I was a (lay) member first encountered proposals for safeguarding procedures: 'But in this church we trust each other!' was the angry response. Sadly, those who seek access to vulnerable adults or children for the wrong reasons can be skilled in conveying the kinds of attributes that would lead others to trust them (building primary trust). Systems of checking for safety and suitability are not infallible but they provide an essential institutional framework, which must be combined with vigilance and awareness of risk (see Chapter 4).

The *trusting instinct* refers to an individual's propensity to trust. Human social life is only possible because of a certain willingness to trust, and each of us is formed through our family and childhood experiences to have a greater or lesser readiness to place our trust in others. There will be those who, for whatever reason, find it difficult to trust us and who lose trust in us over (what may seem) trivial matters. Working with people and groups in a variety of high- and low-trust relationships is part and parcel of the pastoral task.

All congregations have people who struggle to trust others. One of the tragedies of child abuse is that it can have a long-lasting impact in this area. It is part of the Church's task to address the needs of those victims of abuse whose very experience of the Church has made it extremely difficult for them to trust. Counselling and 'authorized listening' can provide real help, and often what a victim wants most of all is to know that their situation has been heard and taken seriously by the Church.

My own ministry in Brussels involved caring for a large community of Rwandans who migrated to Belgium following the genocide. It was part of our church's mission to help them find their feet in a new and alien society. I met and talked with people who had witnessed and suffered the most appalling atrocities and who bore the scars of the experiences on their own minds and bodies. Yet by a combination of divine grace and human resilience their faith and trust in God and in others had survived and indeed grown. I write of their experience not in any sense as 'normative' but simply as evidence of what kind of psychological rebuilding is sometimes possible.

The final area of trust relates to *a trust culture*. In the same way that the trusting impulse is a product of personal biography, so a trust culture is the product of social histories at a local or national level. As the established church, the Church of England is one of the actors that shapes national culture through its presence in every community, the pronouncements of its archbishops and bishops, and even through the unspoken witness of its impressive built heritage. As we have suggested, although there is a significant culture of suspicion, major national institutions and professions (the police, the civil service, the health service, the Church) are trusted in the UK to a high degree. This is something for which we should be more thankful. Mainland Britain has not experienced invasion or civil war for many centuries, and has been spared dictatorship and serious mafia influence or public corruption. Few countries in Europe, let alone the rest of the world, have been so fortunate.

The local church has its own micro-culture. It can and should be a community of high trust with a delightful set of mainly unconscious norms and values that regulate, grant, meet, return and reciprocate trust. Occasionally, things happen in local churches that damage trust – maybe a bad property decision, financial mismanagement or impropriety. Churches are right to take infidelity seriously, since a failure of trust in the closest of relationships casts doubt on trustworthiness in less significant relationships and responsibilities.

Building a trust culture is central to the work of the local minister. He or she does this through modelling personal integrity, good judgement, wise interventions and careful attention to the appointment of lay officers. Where there has been a recent breach of trust, healing of the church's life is needed. Where mistakes and hurts linger from the past a wise incumbent will take a good deal of time to listen to the stories, find sensitive ways of addressing matters in prayer, and help the community to move forward.[17]

Conclusion

We live in a culture that encourages suspicion, especially of those in authority. Such a culture tends to generate 'controls' on people that only make us more suspicious. The Church and its clergy need to find ways of demonstrating trustworthiness that are genuinely effective. Trust involves confidence, but is more than confidence. According to Stzompka's model of trust, we need to build primary trust, secondary trust, the trusting impulse and trust culture. The Church as God intends it has faith and trust at its heart. Being a human institution, sometimes things happen that

---

[17] See for instance the books, resources and programmes offered by Russ Parker and Acorn Christian Healing Trust on 'Healing wounded churches', www.acornchristian.org/news/healing-wounded-churches

erode or damage trust. Contributing to the building and rebuilding of the Church as a high-trust community is central to Christian ministry. High-trust church communities are delightful places where people love to belong and that are released to be more effective in the mission of God.

References

Church of England, *Canons of the Church of England*, 7th edn, https://www.churchofengland.org/about-us/structure/churchlawlegis/canons/canons-7th-edition.aspx>

Church of England, *Clergy Discipline Measure*, <https://www.churchofengland.org/media/2192477/cdm%202003%20amended%20by%20cd%28a%29m%20as%20published%20feb%202014.pdf>

Covey, S. R., *The Seven Habits of Highly Effective People: Powerful Lessons in Personal Change*. Free Press, New York, 1989.

England, R., *Leading with Trust*. Grove Books, Cambridge, 2015.

Fukuyama, F., *Trust: The Social Virtues and the Creation of Prosperity*. The Free Press, New York, 1995.

Giddens, A., *The Third Way*. Polity Press, Cambridge, 1998.

Harrison, J., Innes, R. and van Zwanenberg, T., *Rebuilding Trust in Healthcare*. Radcliffe Medical Press, Abingdon, 2003.

Misztal, B., *Trust in Modern Societies*. Basil Blackwell, Oxford, 1996.

O'Neil, O., *A Question of Trust: The BBC Reith Lectures 2002*. Cambridge University Press, Cambridge, 2002.

Putnam, R., 'Bowling alone: America's declining social capital', *Journal of Democracy*, 1995, 6:65–78.

Sztompka, P., *Trust: A Sociological Theory*. Cambridge University Press, Cambridge, 1999.

Williams, R., *Lost Icons*, Continuum, London, 2000.

12

Faithful servants in a complex age

———•◦•———

JAMIE HARRISON

They are to be messengers, watchmen and stewards of the Lord.
(The Ordinal)

The way to please Him is to feed my flock diligently and
faithfully, since our Saviour hath made that the argument of
a Pastor's love. (George Herbert)

I adore simple pleasures. They are the last refuge of the
complex. (Oscar Wilde)

It is always informative to look back to discern what God might
have been saying to his Church, not least the Church of England and her clergy. George Herbert (1593-1633) most probably
wrote his book *A Priest to the Temple, or, The Country Parson,
his Character, and Rule of Holy Life* during the last 12 months of
his life.[1] The manuscript was kept safe by friends and published
20 years later in 1652, some ten years before the arrival of the
1662 *Book of Common Prayer*. In this work, commonly termed
The Country Parson, Herbert laid out his own set of guidelines
for conduct. In all there are 37 brief chapters, with an introduction
and prayers for before and after a sermon as appendices. Topics
covered include praying, preaching, catechizing, blessing, giving,
visiting and disciplining, as well as the practical concerns of
the church building, the parsonage, and how to deal with the

---

[1] Herbert, G., *A Priest to the Temple, or, The Country Parson, his Character, and Rule of
Holy Life*. Maxey and Garthwait, St Paul's, London, 1652.

churchwardens! It is the seventeenth-century equivalent of our *Guidelines*, without (of course) the benefit of a drafting committee, or convocations to give approval.

By the time Herbert's book finally appeared, Anthony Russell reminds us, Oliver Cromwell was in power and the Anglican Church almost eclipsed, its ministers forced to practise, preach and conduct services in secret. In the Preface to the Second Edition of *A Priest to the Temple*, which appeared some 11 years after the Restoration, Barnabas Oley looked back to the dark days of the Commonwealth and 'congratulated himself on his courage . . . in publishing such a book at a time "when violence was at the height"'. Russell sees this as Oley's attempt to encourage a new cohort of younger clergy to emulate George Herbert's quality of religious life.[2] These were those 'not born before the troubles broke forth' and could be reminded of 'what a halcyon calm, a blessed time of peace, this Church of England had for many years, above all the churches in the world beside'.[3]

Context is everything

Reflecting on our own complex times, we can be tempted to hark back to a 'simpler' age. If only we could return to those 'halcyon days', not so much to Herbert's rural pastoral ministry of 1632, but perhaps to another, more recent era, when the Church was taken more seriously and clergy properly respected. 'Anyone for Barchester?' you might ask.[4] Or perhaps not . . .

In the parallel world I inhabit, that of the National Health Service, similar feelings can arise. 'Can we not return to real family doctoring and proper personal care?' If the founding of the NHS in 1948 is seen as a high-water mark (and it was certainly a brave and prophetic act), then not all it replaced was bad, nor is all that it has become good, and vice versa. First published in 1967, John Berger's

---

[2] Russell, A., *The Country Parson*. SPCK, London, 1993, p. 53.
[3] Oley, B., Preface to the Second Edition, *A Priest to the Temple*. London, 1671.
[4] Trollope, A., *Barchester Towers*. Longmans, London, 1857.

wonderful study of a country GP, *A Fortunate Man*, tells the story of Dr John Sassall as he, along with his patients, accommodates to the brave new world of post-1948 (where penicillin was still the wonder discovery). As the back cover announces, 'no other book has offered such a close and passionate investigation of the roles doctors play in their society'.[5] For once, such comments are not misplaced. Berger, and his photographer Jean Mohr, were drawn into the common-place, of what it meant to be an intimate player in a close-knit community, where words like professional commitment and faithfulness were assumed. It was a time when the GP attended every home birth, a time of optimism that modern medicine might soon cure everything, and, in so doing, put itself out of business.

Yet that world feels almost as far away from today's as does Trollope's, never mind Herbert's. We are reminded that context is everything, and that change – sometimes slow and sometimes rapid – is a constant; that what we thought we were getting into may not be what we find at the end. Such fluctuations and fractures can catch us out, depress us or energize us.

What is good(-enough)?

John Berger senses that Dr Sassal, his 'fortunate man', is regarded by his patients as a good doctor – in the way he organizes his practice, the facilities he offers, his use of clinical skills – but that he is probably somewhat underrated. For Berger, these patients may not realize how lucky they are. But, he says, in a sense this is inevitable. 'Only the most self-conscious consider it lucky to have their elementary needs met. And it is on a very basic, elementary level that he is judged a good doctor.'[6]

For the family doctor, as much as the parish cleric, there can be a constant set of questions humming at the back of the mind.

---

[5] Berger, J., *A Fortunate Man: The Story of a Country Doctor*. Random House, New York, 1997, back cover.
[6] Berger, *A Fortunate Man*, pp. 62–3.

'How am I doing?' 'Am I good enough?' 'Am I keeping up?' To some degree these are impossible questions to answer properly. Friends, family members, colleagues, patients/parishioners can all give an answer, although we rarely ask them, and may not believe them anyway. Today's world of medicine has formal mechanisms to gain feedback from those we treat and those with whom we work. Such 'multi-source feedback' has its place, but less clearly so in small teams, such as some general practices, where folk know one another, and can guess who must have filled in the form. I'm not convinced how well it would work for clergy . . .

The traditional way for professionals to gauge what they do has been through reflecting on historic guidance. For doctors this began as the Hippocratic oath, continued through a range of ethical statements and (in the UK) became embedded in the General Medical Council's *Good Medical Practice.* Here the themes of trust, safety, quality, communication, teamwork, knowledge, skills and performance are fleshed out and examined in context.[7] So how might it work for the clergy? The Ordinal, the 39 Articles of Religion and the Canons have their place, as do the Holy Scriptures. We might add George Herbert into the mix too. But, as for medicine's older texts, these documents were clearly written for a different age and sensibility. The Guidelines offer another, more contemporary and sustaining response. For they speak into a context described by Justin Welby in the Foreword to this book as 'a complex age with shifting boundaries – sexual, relational, legal and ecclesial' where 'clarity around expectations is immensely helpful'.

So are guidelines enough?

And yet any set of guidelines is only as good as its formulators, and the effectiveness of such guidance only as good as its reception

---

[7] General Medical Council, *Good Medical Practice.* General Medical Council, London, 2013, <www.gmc-uk.org/guidance/good_medical_practice.asp>

and application. To some degree one could argue that good practitioners don't need guidelines and poor ones won't follow them. Or I am I being too cynical? Well-framed guidelines set out the boundaries and frameworks for good practice, and remind everyone what is possible and what could and should be done. Yet, as with *Good Medical Practice*, the key element for success is the commitment of the professional to the task, that sense of inner connectedness with, and to, the job (or vocation) in hand. So guidelines can take you a long way, but not all the way. Otherwise we would not need the General Medical Council or the Clergy Discipline Commission.

Or putting this in a different register, can we talk about faithfulness? In faithful response to a calling, however described and understood, professionals gain traction and validity, and – in Berger's words – are noted by those they serve as 'good'. This faithfulness is most likely to be 'underrated', not well recognized or valued. It is the experience of family doctors and parish clergy that their presence and availability is assumed, although in more recent times GPs have chosen to be more protective of their boundaries. As we noted back in 1998,

> The myth of constant availability could only be maintained when the doctor knew that patients would not act as if it were true. One GP recently quipped that 'doctors offered everything on the basis that patients would not ask too much'.[8]

Growing professionalism

With regard to the rural church, Timothy Jenkins makes the point that the nineteenth century saw major changes in the role of the clergy. Religious movements and reforms led to a separation of

---

[8] Harrison, J. and Innes, R., *Medical Vocation and Generation X*. Grove Books, Cambridge, 1997, pp. 10–11.

interests and a new pattern of vocation emerging, instanced by 'the withdrawal of the parish church from direct involvement in agriculture, formerly represented by tithes and glebe farms; the increased emphasis upon the sacred role of the priest; and the growing "professionalism" of the clergy'.[9] This direction of travel has proved to be a mixed blessing for doctors and clergy alike, where becoming more specialized in role, at a time of losing close involvement in everyday communities, can lead to a form of 'isolated professionalism'.

Jenkins notes that, as with the clergy themselves, the Church as an institution has become more professional. It has also, until recently at least, concentrated its forces on the cities. Reports on the rural church have begun to offer new ideas and energy, notably *Faith in the Countryside* (1990) and the recent *Released for Mission: Growing the Rural Church*.[10] Yet ministry in both rural and city settings, and everywhere in between, remains increasingly complex, whether it be in relation to multi-church and multi-benefice contexts, or the increasingly diverse and dislocated urban 'communities', or the busyness and caution of the average parishioner.

Here faithful professionalism remains both challenge and source of pride. It brings with it rights and responsibilities, and the acceptance of proper systems of governance. It requires humility, competence, responsiveness and accessibility. Professionals need to keep up to date, be flexible and good team workers, and be those who willingly follow a code of conduct.[11]

---

[9] Jenkins, T., *Religion in English Everyday Life: An Ethnographic Approach*. Berghahn Books, Oxford, 1999, pp. 60–1.

[10] Archbishops' Commission on Rural Areas, *Faith in the Countryside*. Churchman Publishing Ltd, London, 1990; Archbishops' Council, *Released for Mission: Growing the Rural Church: GS Misc 1092*, Church House Publishing, London, 2015, <www.churchofengland. org/media-centre/news/2015/01/released-for-mission,-growing-the-rural-church.aspx>

[11] Harrison, J. and Innes, R., 'The end of certainty: professionalism revisited', in Harrison, J. and van Zwanenberg, T., *Clinical Governance in Primary Care*, 2nd edn. Radcliffe Medical Press, Oxford, 2004, p. 237.

Only connect . . .[12]

Guidelines exists to help and not to hinder, to provide supportive wisdom and not to undermine. It offers the 14 Guidelines themselves, plus helpful theological reflection and advice on further reading. In this book, the intention has been to offer a way into the Guidelines that is realistic and possible. We have sought to guide folk in a way that is not fussy or over-prescriptive; rather we want clergy to try things out and see what is do-able for them.

There is no doubt that, in order to be faithful servants of the Church of Jesus Christ, clergy must be safe and trustworthy, and the Guidelines make that clear. These areas are non-negotiable. Beyond that, a range of possibilities opens up, and as editors we have taken the liberty of asking our contributors for responses that focus on particular themes or sub-themes. As we stated at the beginning, this book is not an explanation or exegesis of the Guidelines, neither is it a comprehensive engagement with every jot or tittle.

In asking for contributions on witness, blessing, leadership, imagination, living in the private and public sphere, and keeping well, it was not our intention to narrow down the Guidelines sections into these particular ways of being and doing. It is for others to flesh out those wider fields, and the literature, say, on mission and evangelism or healing or learning and teaching is well worth a look.

Faithful servants in a complex age

In the final analysis, in the suspicious, complex, complicated and often turbulent world of today, we decided to follow Oscar Wilde's advice and recommend the value of simple pleasures, of doing

---

[12] E. M. Forster's famous injunction on the title page of his novel *Howard's End*, first published in 1910.

simple things well, and of seeking to be faithful servants. In his poem 'Love (III)' quoted in the Afterword to this book, George Herbert paints a picture in words of Christ's invitation of love, where, as the poem progresses, our response becomes that of grateful service in return. In *The Country Parson* Herbert lays out how that service might be seen, much in the way *Guidelines* seeks to do. There is much overlap; perhaps that is not too surprising.

At a time of rapid technological and societal change, clergy continue to be a source of stability and hope. As they share Christ with others, as they pray, visit, offer blessing and words of healing, as well as the more 'professional' stuff, they witness to the One who is 'all in all'. Clergy have a noble calling. May they live it with love, devotion and fortitude, so that at the end of their lives they can say with St Paul, 'I have fought the good fight, I have finished the race. From now on there is reserved for me the crown of righteousness' (2 Timothy 4.7–8).

References

Archbishops' Commission on Rural Areas, *Faith in the Countryside*. Churchman Publishing Ltd, London, 1990.

Archbishops' Council, *Released for Mission: Growing the Rural Church: GS Misc 1092*, Church House Publishing, London, 2015, <https://www.churchofengland.org/media-centre/news/2015/01/released-for-mission,-growing-the-rural-church.aspx>

Berger, J., *A Fortunate Man: The Story of a Country Doctor*. Random House, New York, 1997.

Forster, E. M., *Howard's End*. E. Arnold, London, 1910.

General Medical Council, *Good Medical Practice*. General Medical Council, London, 2013, <www.gmc-uk.org/guidance/good_medical_practice.asp>

Harrison, J. and Innes, R., *Medical Vocation and Generation X*. Grove Books, Cambridge, 1997.

Harrison, J. and van Zwanenberg, T., *Clinical Governance in Primary Care*, 2nd edn. Radcliffe Medical Press, Oxford, 2004.

Herbert, G., *A Priest to the Temple, or, The Country Parson, his Character, and Rule of Holy Life*. Maxey and Garthwait, St Paul's, London, 1652.

Jenkins, T., *Religion in English Everyday Life: An Ethnographic Approach*. Berghahn Books, Oxford, 1999.

Oley, B., Preface to the Second Edition, *A Priest to the Temple*. St Paul's, London, 1671.

Russell, A., *The Clerical Profession*. SPCK, London, 1980.

Russell, A., *The Country Parson*. SPCK, London, 1993.

Trollope, A., *Barchester Towers*. Longmans, London, 1857.

Afterword

JAMIE HARRISON AND ROBERT INNES

It is only as we deepen our understanding of the faithfulness of God that we ourselves become more faithful. In heeding God's call to us to follow, as faithful servants we learn the ways of grace and trust; we become more Christ-like; we take on the new nature; we are redeemed.

George Herbert (1593–1633) knew this keenly, and as he entered the last year of his all too brief life, he wrote of God's faithfulness and forgiveness. This sensibility was also a feature of the life of Ruth Etchells (1931–2012), to whom this book is dedicated. In her last days, she spoke of a God who had remained faithful to her, despite all that had happened in her life: in the trials, difficulties and disappointments, as well as in the joys and the hopes fulfilled.

Ruth taught courses on theology and literature at Durham University. She also understood what it meant to struggle, to forgive and to be forgiven. Of Herbert's poems she wrote:

> The final purpose of Herbert's verse is joy; joy in all that God gives to his creation, joy in the acts of God in human history, joy most of all in the perfect forgiveness and peace that God gives in the struggling heart, through his act of saving love in his Son, Jesus Christ.[1]

And for Herbert, it was indeed Love's call that both bought, and brought, the response of faith, and of faithful service:

---

[1] Etchells, R., *A Selection of Poems by George Herbert: The Lenten Poet, Exploring his Pilgrimage of Faith*. Lion Publishing, Tring, 1988, p. 28.

'Love III'

Love bade me welcome: yet my soul drew back
    Guiltie of dust and sinne.
But quick-ey'd Love, observing me grow slack
    From my first entrance in,
Drew nearer to me, sweetly questioning,
    If I lack'd any thing.

A guest, I answer'd, worthy to be here:
    Love said, You shall be he.
I the unkinde, ungratefull? Ah my deare,
    I cannot look on thee.
Love took my hand, and smiling did reply,
    Who made the eyes but I?

Truth Lord, but I have marr'd them: let my shame
    Go where it doth deserve.
And know you not, sayes Love, who bore the blame?
    My deare, then I will serve.
You must sit down, sayes Love, and taste my meat:
    So I did sit and eat.[2]

---

[2] Herbert, G., 'Love III' from *The Temple*. London, 1633.

Appendix
Guidelines for the professional conduct of the clergy[1]

-------•·●·•-------

Calling

1   Priests are to set the example of the Good Shepherd always before them . . .

1.1   The three orders of ordained ministry play a central role in the mission of the Church which Jesus Christ entrusted to his Apostles, to 'go and make disciples of all nations, baptizing them in the name of the Father and of the Son and of the Holy Spirit, teaching them to observe all that I have commanded you' (Matthew 28.19-20).

1.2   Ordained ministers bear the privilege and responsibility of being servants and leaders in the ministry of the Church. As pastors, spiritual guides and representatives of the Christian faith, they are in a position of trust in their relationships with those for whom they have pastoral care.

1.3   The compassion, care and kindness of the Good Shepherd should be the hallmarks of the clergy. Unworthy behaviour disgraces the Church and undermines the gospel.

1.4   All personal and professional conduct is bounded by law and legal sanction. For the clergy, who swear the Oaths of Canonical Obedience and Allegiance, and make the Declaration of Assent, this will include ecclesiastical law as well as secular law. Thus nothing in these Guidelines should be

---

[1] The Convocations of Canterbury and York, 'Guidelines for the professional conduct of the clergy', in *Guidelines for the Professional Conduct of the Clergy*, rev. edn, Church House Publishing, London, 2015. © The Archbishops Council, 2015. Used by permission. <copyright@churchofengland.org.uk>

read as suggesting that clergy stand outside the rule of criminal or civil law. Indeed, any concern about possible criminal behaviour, and in particular any information about abuse or risk of abuse will be reported by the Church authorities to the police.

Care

2   **They are to sustain the community of the faithful . . .**

2.1   Caring for one another is the responsibility of the whole Church and is an extension of the justice and love of the Incarnate God disclosed in Jesus Christ. Compassion is essential to pastoral care. The clergy should enable other members of the worshipping community to share in this pastoral care, ensuring that they are recruited safely, and have the appropriate training and supervision for the tasks involved, including current training in safeguarding in accordance with the guidance issued by the House of Bishops. (See also 2.9)

Clergy should seek to ensure that churchwardens, PCCs and the wider congregation understand their responsibilities and roles in making every church a safe place for all.

2.2   In their ministry, pastoral care and working relationships, the clergy should offer equal respect and opportunity to all. They should be unbiased in their exercise of pastoral care, especially when caring for one party in a dispute between two or more people. In some cases they may need to ask another appropriate person to provide pastoral care to one of the parties.

2.3   The clergy should discern and acknowledge their own limitations of time, competence and skill. They will need to seek support, help and appropriate training and, on occasion, to refer to specialist agencies. The clergy should be aware of the help available from accredited agencies so that it can be commended where appropriate.

2.4   Clergy should always be conscious of the power dynamics involved in their pastoral care, noting both the position of trust which they hold and the power which they exercise. See also Sections 12 and 14.

2.5 The distinctions between the various roles in which the clergy exercise oversight and care are always to be recognized and acknowledged. Ministers need to be clear with those with whom they are dealing. At no time should they provide formal counselling for those in their pastoral care, even when they are accredited as counsellors in other settings. Those who wish to work as accredited counsellors should seek appropriate advice about how to maintain proper boundaries between this and their role as ordained ministers.

2.6 Similarly, where the clergy are supervising employed members of staff, or mentoring or coaching church members, there needs to be absolute clarity about the role in which they are engaging with them. The responsibility for pastoral care must not be confused with any other role.

2.7 There is risk in all pastoral work. The appropriateness of visiting and being visited alone, especially at night, needs to be assessed with care. The same assessment should also apply to other 'out of hours' contact (especially through telephone calls and social media).

Consideration should be given to:
- the place of the meeting;
- the proximity of other people;
- the arrangement of furniture and lighting; and
- the dress of the minister, appropriate to the context

– which are important considerations in pastoral care. The perceptions of others need to be considered at all times, taking particular care to assess the extent to which others may experience or perceive behaviour to be inappropriate.

At times it may be appropriate to advise a third party in advance of any appointments which have been made. Keeping accurate records of appointments is helpful and good practice.

2.8 It is essential in pastoral care to acknowledge appropriate physical, sexual, emotional and psychological boundaries. Inappropriate touching or gestures of affection are to be avoided. The clergy need to be aware of what is appropriate when meeting people from different cultural traditions.

2.9 The clergy should be aware of the dangers of dependency in pastoral relationships. Manipulation, competitiveness or collusion on either side of the pastoral encounter should be avoided. Self-awareness should be part of the relationship. The responsibility for maintaining appropriate boundaries always rests with the clergy, however difficult or challenging the pastoral relationship may prove to be.

2.10 The clergy must always put first the interests of those for whom they are pastorally responsible, and act to protect them even where this requires them to override personal and professional loyalties. It is their duty to raise concerns where they believe that someone's safety or care is being compromised by the practice of colleagues, or by those in authority, or by the systems, policies or procedures with which they are expected to work. They must also encourage and support the development of a culture in which they and their colleagues can raise concerns openly and honestly. Those in authority should listen carefully to their concerns and act upon them where they are justified, enabling those who have the best interests of others at heart to raise concerns without fear of detriment to themselves.

2.11 The clergy are required to have appropriate and current training in safeguarding children and vulnerable adults. Failure to participate may result in action being taken under the Clergy Discipline Measure. The Church of England's national and diocesan policies, guidelines and requirements must be known and observed. If they become aware that someone known to have a conviction for offences against children or vulnerable adults attends their church, they must follow the guidelines for ministering to such offenders.

2.12 Clergy should be clear about the circumstances in which information about abuse of all forms, or the risk of abuse, must be reported to the statutory authorities (that is, the police or local authority children's or adult services). Children or adults who provide information about abuse need to know that their concerns will be taken seriously and that the clergy will work with them in making the referral, in order that a proper investigation can be undertaken and appropriate help be obtained.

2.13 It is essential that clergy maintain an accurate and factual written record of any safeguarding concerns or actions. They should be aware of the dangers of glossing over the conduct of fellow clergy, or even of collusion with it.

2.14 All the clergy should be aware of the circumstances in which information can and should be disclosed to third parties. To that end, they should refer to the national and diocesan safeguarding policies. When preparing for such a disclosure, the clergy should seek appropriate legal and other specialist advice, for example from the Diocesan Safeguarding Adviser. Whenever a safeguarding referral is made, clergy should always inform the Diocesan Safeguarding Adviser.

2.15 Similar requirements apply if the conduct of a colleague appears inappropriate, when advice should always be obtained and action taken.

2.16 The clergy should ensure that all communications they may have with or about children or vulnerable adults are appropriate in their tone and that they comply with relevant national and diocesan policies and guidance. This refers to the use of any means of communication, written, spoken or electronic. Anything published online is public and visible to everyone.

2.17 The clergy should take care to observe appropriate bound-aries between their work and their personal life just as much in the use of social media as in 'real life' encounters. They should recognize the importance of knowing themselves and their own emotional needs. Working with a spiritual director or pastoral supervisor can greatly help the development of this insight, which is difficult to achieve when working alone.

In this context it should be noted that paragraph 5.21 of *Protecting All God's Children* states: 'Clergy should not expose themselves or others to material which is sexually explicit, profane, obscene, harassing, fraudulent, racially offensive, politically inflammatory, defamatory or in violation of any British, European or international law.'

Reconciliation

3   **They are to teach and to admonish, to feed and provide for his family . . .**

3.1   The ministry of reconciliation, as an extension of Jesus' own ministry, lies at the heart of this vocation. It is to be exercised gently, patiently and undergirded by mutual trust. It may include spiritual or godly counsel as appropriate and as requested by those concerned; it may include mediation between those who have found themselves at enmity with one another.

3.2   Where it is freely sought by a penitent, a priest may exercise the formal ministry of absolution as described in Canon B 29.

3.3   The ministry of absolution may only be exercised by the minister who has the cure of souls of the place in question or by another priest with that minister's permission, or by a priest who is authorized by law to exercise ministry in that place without being subject to the control of the minister who has the cure of souls (e.g. a priest who is licensed to exercise ministry under the Extra-Parochial Ministry Measure 1967). This rule is subject to an exception that permits a priest to exercise the ministry of absolution any-where in respect of a person who is in danger of death or if there is 'some urgent or weighty cause' (See Canon B 29.4)

3.4 Before undertaking the ministry of absolution a priest should receive appropriate training and be familiar with any guidelines published by the House of Bishops that relate to the exercise of this ministry.

3.5 A clear distinction must be made between pastoral con-versations and a confession that is made in the context of the ministry of absolution. Where such a confession is to be made both the priest and the penitent should be clear that that is the case. If a penitent makes a confession with the intention of receiving absolution the priest is forbidden (by the unrepealed *Proviso* to Canon 113 of the Code of 1603) to reveal or make known to any person what has been confessed. This requirement of absolute confidentiality applies even after the death of the penitent.

3.6 If, in the context of such a confession, the penitent discloses that he or she has committed a serious crime, such as the abuse of children or vulnerable adults, the priest must require the penitent to report his or her conduct to the police or other statutory authority. If the penitent refuses to do so the priest should withhold absolution.

3.7 The canonical duty of absolute confidentiality does not apply to anything that is said outside the context of such a confession. In particular, if information about abuse that was disclosed when seeking the ministry of absolution is repeated by the penitent outside that context the priest must follow the established procedures for reporting abuse of children or vulnerable adults.

3.8 However confidentiality extends far beyond the specific situation of the ministry of absolution. People have to be able to trust clergy with their stories, their fears, and espe-cially their confidences. The duty of confidentiality relating to the ministry of absolution sets a standard for our ministry against which all other instances should be set and judged. Those to whom we minister must know that they can depend upon us not to disclose information which they have shared with us in confidence.

Note: *The text of this section reflects the current legal position in relation to the ministry of absolution, arising from the unrepealed proviso to Canon 113 of the Code of 1603. In September 2014 the Archbishops' Council decided to commission further theological and legal work to enable it to review, in consultation with the House of Bishops, the purpose and effect of the proviso to the Canon of 1603, with a view to enabling the General Synod to decide whether it wished to amend it.*

Mission

4   **They are to tell the story of God's love . . .**

4.1   Mission belongs to the whole church worldwide and is a primary calling of the clergy. Parish priests are charged with the 'cure of souls' not solely the chaplaincy of congregations. As such, they have a clear responsibility, with their people, to develop appropriate practices of mission and evangelism in their parish, network or other context.

4.2   The clergy should ensure that services are thoughtfully and thoroughly prepared, matching the need and culture of the parish or institution within the Anglican tradition. Where appropriate, they should involve others in leading worship, having ensured that they are equipped to do so, by providing training and preparation as necessary to support them.

4.3   The clergy should ensure that appropriate and accessible courses and discussion groups on all aspects of the Christian faith are available at regular intervals to parishioners seeking to explore, deepen or renew their faith.

4.4   Suitable preparation for Baptism, Confirmation and Marriage is a primary responsibility for the clergy.

4.5   The clergy should recognize, affirm and encourage the ministry and witness of lay people. This should include acknowledging their mission in workplaces and communities.

4.6   All schools, along with other institutions within a parish, may provide opportunities for mission and ministry, and a church school is a particular responsibility for the clergy. The clergy should seek to enhance opportunities for themselves and appropriately gifted and trained laity to contribute to the worship, religious education, pastoral care and governance in local schools and colleges.

4.7   In an increasingly 'mixed economy' Church, which fosters pioneer ordained ministry and Fresh Expressions of Church as well as traditional parish ministry and mission, ministers who lead such pioneering mission are subject to the same call, responsibility and accountability.

Ministry at times of deepest need

5   **They are to bless the people in God's name ...**

5.1   The clergy have a particular responsibility to minister sensitively and effectively to the sick, the dying and the bereaved. Ministry to those near to death should never be delayed.

5.2   The clergy should be familiar with and follow the current House of Bishops' *Guidelines for Good Practice in the Healing Ministry*. Existing diocesan regulations should be followed. Professional boundaries with health care professionals and chaplaincies should be observed. All reasonable steps should be taken to ensure the safety of the person receiving the healing ministry, including by ensuring that satisfactory arrangements are in place for training and accountability for those undertaking this ministry.

5.3   The clergy should be aware of and respect the boundaries between the ministry of healing and the deliverance ministry. People have a right to know what is being provided and how they will be ministered to: no one should be ministered to against their will.

5.4 Deliverance is an area of ministry where particular caution needs to be exercised, especially when ministering to someone who is in a disturbed state. The current House of Bishops' guidelines on the deliverance ministry which are known as The House of Bishops' *Guidelines for Good Practice in the Deliverance Ministry 1975* (revised 2012) should be followed and cases referred to the diocesan advisers for the deliverance ministry when necessary. The advisers' special expertise should be used in order to help as effectively as possible those who think they need this ministry.

5.5 The ministry of exorcism and deliverance may only be exercised by priests who have been specifically and personally authorized by the bishop, normally for each instance of such a ministry. If this ministry is sought in connection with a child or vulnerable adults, the Diocesan Safeguarding Adviser must be involved and may need to ensure that a referral to the statutory authorities is made, in accordance with national and diocesan safeguarding policies.

Servant Leadership

6 **Guided by the Spirit, they are to discern and foster the gifts of all God's people . . .**

6.1 The clergy are called to servant ministry and leadership within the Church and the wider community.

6.2 They should develop this gift of leadership within their own ministry through prayer and training, being aware of their own natural leadership style.

6.3 The clergy should recognize and affirm lay ministry that already exists and encourage new ministries, both lay and ordained. They should be ready to assist others in discerning and fulfilling their vocation. They should actively prompt and encourage new vocations in the Church and in the world.

6.4   At times as we seek to hear God's call for the Church in this generation, the clergy will hold different views. However, all debate should be had in a spirit of respect and love, and ministers should always be willing to work with each other, whatever views are held on current topics of debate.

6.5   The clergy should promote good ecumenical relationships and encourage respect for all people of good will.

6.6   Upon resignation or retirement, the clergy should relinquish their responsibilities and should cease professional relationships with those formerly under their pastoral care. Any exception to this guideline should be formally negotiated with the bishop.

6.7   Having resigned or retired, the clergy may not minister in a former church, parish or institution unless invited by the clergy with pastoral oversight or with their express permission. Ministry in retirement is subject to the bishop granting a Licence or Permission To Officiate, and subject to the completion of safeguarding clearance and training.

Learning and Teaching

7   **Will you be diligent in prayer, in reading Holy Scripture, and in all studies . . . ?**

7.1   The given daily prayer of the Church (the Daily Office) is one of the essential foundations of confident ministry centred on Christ, using the resources of the Church such as the *Book of Common Prayer*, *Common Worship*, or other authorized forms of the office.

7.2   The life of prayer, although personal, includes the praise and prayer offered in Christ's name in his church, both on earth and in heaven. Clergy should therefore seek to offer the daily prayer of the church with other members of the community in which they serve.

7.3   To pray for others in thanksgiving for the benefits of Christ is a common duty of Christians, and is a particular privilege of the ordained ministry. To intercede whether in public or in private belongs to the ways God accomplishes in his church that which he wills.

7.4 The use of conversation with a chosen companion such as a spiritual guide or with others sharing the ordained ministry is commended, recognizing the different ways in which God has called his people to relate to him, and enabled them to do so.

7.5 It is part of the mission of the clergy to teach those whom they serve both the ways and the delight of prayer, being open to learning these things as they do so.

7.6 Continued theological learning is an essential discipline for preaching and teaching, as well as for personal growth.

7.7 The clergy should set aside time for continuing ministerial education and development, including the consideration of contemporary issues and theological developments, so that their faith engages with the perceptions and concerns of this generation.

7.8 Keeping abreast of a whole variety of communicating skills is crucial to the effective and ongoing proclamation of the gospel.

7.9 Part of the clerical vocation in both preaching and teaching is a prayerful openness to being prophetic and challenging as well as encouraging and illuminating.

7.10 Great care should be taken that illustrative material from personal experience does not involve any breach of confidentiality.

Faith

8 **Do you accept the Holy Scriptures as revealing all things necessary for eternal salvation . . . ?**

8.1 The clergy are required to make the Declaration of Assent (contained in Canon C 15) at their ordination, and at the inauguration of any new ministry within the Church of

England. All should ensure that they know and understand the significance of the statements to which they have publicly given their assent, and that they can accordingly only use the forms of service authorized or allowed to be used in the Church of England.

8.2 The basis of the Church of England's understanding of doctrine and of the sacraments is set out in the Declaration of Assent, and the Preface which precedes it. The Church's clergy should uphold this understanding, having declared their commitment to it formally and publicly at the start of their ministry.

8.3 Ministers who for whatever reason find that they are unable any longer in conscience to believe, hold or teach the Christian faith as the Church of England has received it, should seek advice and help in deciding whether or not they should continue to exercise a public ministry in which they represent the Church.

Public Ministry

9 **Will you . . . strive to be an instrument of God's peace in the Church and in the world?**

9.1 The reputation of the Church in the community depends to a great extent on the integrity and example of its clergy, who should recognize their role as public representatives of the Church. Their lives should enhance and embody the communication of the gospel.

9.2 The clergy should ensure a reasonable level of availability and accessibility to those for whom they have a pastoral care. A prompt and gracious response to all requests for help demonstrates care. This response should be in the context of appropriate boundaries, so as not to put at risk the clergy, members of their household, or the Church.

9.3 Reconciliation lies at the heart of the gospel: 'God was in Christ reconciling the world to himself' (*2 Corinthians 5.19*).

The clergy should promote reconciliation in the Church and in the world wherever there are divisions, including those which exist between people of different faiths.

9.4 The call of the clergy to be servants to the community should include their prophetic ministry to those in spiritual and moral danger.

9.5 It is appropriate for the clergy to play a positive part in civic society and politics, promoting the kingdom values of justice, integrity and peace in public life, calling attention to the needs of the poor and to the godly stewardship of the world's resources.

9.6 Ministers must not be members or active supporters of any political party or other organization whose constitution, policies, objectives, activities or public statements are incompatible with the teaching of the Church of England, as defined by the House of Bishops, in relation to the equality of persons or groups of different races.

9.7 There are a number of situations where the clergy may have a conflict of interest and they should declare it, whenever that is appropriate, withdrawing from the situation if required. It is a delusion to think we can be impartial when there is a conflict of interest.

Life and Conduct

10 **Will you . . . fashion your own life and that of your household according to the way of Christ . . . ?**

10.1 The clergy are called to an exemplary standard of moral behaviour. This goes beyond what is legally acceptable: a distinction can be made between what is legal and what is morally acceptable. There is no separation between the public and home life of the clergy: at all times and in all places they should manifest the highest standards of personal conduct.

10.2 The clergy should set an example of integrity in relationships, and faithfulness in marriage. Marital infidelity is regarded as 'unbecoming or inappropriate conduct' for the purposes of the Clergy Discipline Measure. The House of Bishops' *Marriage: A Teaching Document* (1999) clearly affirms, 'Sexual intercourse, as an expression of faithful intimacy, properly belongs within marriage exclusively.'

10.3 Those who are called to marriage should never forget that this is also a vocation. It should not be thought to be of secondary importance to their vocation to ministry. Being a parent is likewise a holy calling and so ordained ministry should not take priority over bringing up children with Godly love, care, time and space. Similar considerations may apply to caring for other members of the family.

10.4 All should guard themselves and their family against becoming victims of harmful levels of stress. It is the calling of all Christians, whether married or not, including those with a vocation to celibacy, to take the necessary steps to nurture in holiness their lives, their friendships and their family relationships.

10.5 Good administration enables the work of ministry. Dealing promptly with correspondence and enquiries with efficiency and courtesy is essential.

10.6 The keeping of parochial registers and records to a high standard is legally required.

10.7 The clergy need to ensure that all their financial activities, whether personal or corporate, meet the highest ethical standards. There must be strict boundaries between church finance and personal moneys in order to avoid the possibility of suspicion or impropriety. This will require accurate and careful record keeping of money which is received from others, including Parochial Fees, and a proper audit trail for all money which is to be passed on to third parties including the PCC, the Diocesan Board of Finance and the tax authorities.

10.8 The clergy should never seek any personal advantage or gain by virtue of their clerical position. Those who receive

personal gifts should keep a record in case of later misunderstandings or false accusations.

10.9 The clergy should take care of their physical well-being.
They should not undertake any professional duties when
medically advised against it, and avoid the influence
of alcohol or drugs. Those who find themselves in difficulty with addictions of any kind should seek appropriate
help.

10.10 Blasphemous, violent or offensive language or behaviour is
unacceptable at all times. Clergy should manifest the fruit
of the Spirit: see Galatians 5.22-23.

Discipline

11. Will you ... accept and minister the discipline of this
Church ... ?

11.1 The clergy should know how ecclesiastical law shapes their
exercise of office and ministry, and should respect such
regulations as are put in place by the Church. They should
familiarize themselves with *The Canons of the Church of
England*, and with any regulations made by the bishop of
the diocese in which they serve.

11.2 The authority of churchwardens and lay people elected or
appointed to office in the local church is to be respected
and affirmed.

11.3 The clergy serve under the authority of the bishop both
in the ministry to which they have been appointed, and
in the diocese as a whole. At their ordination and at every
new appointment they take an Oath of Canonical Obedience,
committing themselves to live within the framework provided by scriptures, creeds, historic formularies, canons and
legislation which govern their ministry within the Church
of England.

11.4 They should participate actively in the life and work of
chapter, deanery, archdeaconry, and diocese, giving support

and respect to ordained and lay colleagues and to those who exercise the responsibility of oversight and leadership.

11.5   Any member of the clergy who is arrested for an offence, however minor, and whether or not charges are brought, is required by the Clergy Discipline Measure to report this fact within 28 days to their bishop. However, clergy who are questioned by the police in relation to a possible arrest should also report that fact.

11.6   Any ordained person who is the subject of an allegation of misconduct in relation to a child or vulnerable adult or of domestic abuse, whether in their public ministry or in their home life, must report this fact straight away to their bishop.

11.7   Clergy whose marriages break down and who are divorced, or have an order of judicial separation made against them, on grounds of their adultery, unreasonable behaviour or desertion by them of their spouse can have a penalty under the Clergy Discipline Measure imposed on them as a result. Any member of the clergy who is a party to a divorce petition or an application for an order for judicial separation should therefore obtain legal advice in respect of their position under the Clergy Discipline Measure before any steps are taken in the matrimonial proceedings.

11.8   Clergy are under a duty to inform their bishop when they are divorced, or have an order of judicial separation made against them.

11.9   The highest standards are expected of the clergy in respect of their personal relationships, not least in respect of their relationships with those in their pastoral care. In particular, the clergy must never have sexual or inappropriate relationships with those aged 16 or 17, or vulnerable adults. A breach of this requirement, in addition to being treated as a disciplinary matter, will be referred to the local authority designated officer. In some cases it may constitute a criminal offence. Anyone found guilty of a criminal or disciplinary offence of this kind is likely to be removed from office and referred to the Disclosure and Barring Service which has power to bar them from work with children and/or vulnerable adults.

11.10 Discretion should be used in all forms of communication including when sending messages by email or text, or when visiting social networking sites or blogs, or holding conversations using cameras or microphones via the internet, much of which relies upon insecure forms of data transmission.

It is advisable for clergy to maintain a distinct email address for their ministry which is not shared with others in the household, and email correspondence received should be accessible only to the person to whom it is sent.

Confidentiality in all forms of correspondence must be respected and maintained whether written or electronic.

11.11 The clergy must remember that they are public figures whose opinions when proffered have weight and significance. In using social media ministers should always assume that anything they post or contribute is in the public domain and will be shared. The power of the internet for doing harm as well as good must always be borne carefully in mind and weighed before saying anything which may prove to be damaging to oneself as well as to others.

11.12 Close attention must be given to secure all forms of data, including traditional paper records. In particular, data held on mobile or desktop computing equipment and on mobile devices should have secure passwords and up-to-date security software.

Trust

12 ... remember the greatness of the trust ...

12.1 The development of trust is of primary importance for honest relationships within ministry.

12.2 The clergy are placed in a position of power and authority over others, in pastoral relationships, with lay colleagues, and sometimes with other ministers. In all forms of ministry, in leadership, teaching, preaching and presiding at worship, the clergy should resist all temptation to exercise power inappropriately. This power needs to be used to sustain others and harness their strengths, and not to abuse, bully, manipulate or denigrate.

12.3 Pastoral care should never seek to remove the autonomy given to the individual. In pastoral situations the other party should be allowed the freedom to make decisions that may be mistaken unless children or vulnerable adults are thereby placed at risk in which case the advice of the Diocesan Safeguarding Adviser must be sought.

12.4 The clergy should thankfully acknowledge their own God-given sexuality. They should not seek sexual advantage, emotionally or physically, in the exercise of their ministry.

12.5 A person seeking pastoral guidance and counsel has the right to expect that the minister concerned will not pass on to a third party confidential information so obtained, without their consent or other lawful authority. Exceptions to the general position include information concerning the commission of a crime or other misconduct, where there is a requirement that the information be disclosed. If a minister has grounds for considering that that exception may apply, or that the disclosure reveals a risk to children or vulnerable adults, he or she should consult the diocesan registrar and, in cases involving safeguarding issues, the Diocesan Safeguarding Adviser.

12.6 Unless otherwise agreed, the clergy are accordingly not at liberty to share confidential information with their spouses, family or friends.

12.7 The content and process of a pastoral relationship may need to be shared with certain other people, such as a supervisor or supervisory group, consultant or other involved colleagues. Such sharing needs to be carefully restricted so that it does not involve any breach of confidence.

12.8 It is important to safeguard the right of parishioners to share personal information with one minister and not another. In a team situation, it may be advisable to create a policy to avoid the danger to ministers within a team of being manipulated and divided by the sharing of personal information with one and not another.

12.9 Ministers who handle personal information about individuals are under the same legal obligations to protect that information under the Data Protection Act 1998 as anyone else. When help or advice is being sought, any note-taking should be mutually agreed wherever possible. If notes contain any information about a living individual which is capable of identifying that individual ('personal data') the notes will be subject to the Act. Information about the Act may be found at www.ico.gov.uk

12.10 The minister of a parish is required by law to provide for the publication of the banns of marriage and the solemnisation of holy matrimony for those within their cure, subject to any impediments which may exist in law to their union. Canon B 33 requires the minister to make inquiries as to the existence of any reasons which may prevent the marriage from taking place, and should seek appropriate advice from the diocesan registrar or the civil authorities in any case of doubt. The clergy should also be aware of the House of Bishops' Guidance on the Marriage of Non-EEA (European Economic Area) Nationals, and the requirement to follow that guidance.

12.11 There is much helpful advice in the Faculty Office publication, *Anglican Marriage in England and Wales: A Guide to the Law for the Clergy*. Copies can be purchased from the Faculty Office at 1 The Sanctuary, Westminster, SW1P 3JT.

12.12 It is the duty of every parochial minister to officiate at the funerals or interment of those who die within their cure, or any parishioners or persons whose names are entered on the church electoral roll of their parish whether deceased within their cure or elsewhere. (Canon B 38). This obligation includes not only funeral services which take place at the parish church, but those which are held in a crematorium or cemetery. Others will also be involved in the care of the bereaved, including funeral directors and cemetery and crematorium staff. The clergy should maintain good professional relationships with all such to ensure appropriate care for the relatives of those who have died.

12.13 Ministers must not officiate or otherwise exercise ministry outside the area of the benefice to which they have been instituted or licensed without the consent of the minister with the cure of souls. This is subject to a statutory entitlement of the minister of a parish to perform a funeral service in any crematorium or cemetery that is situated in another parish without consent provided that the deceased died or was resident in the minister's own parish or was on the electoral roll of that parish at the time of his or her death.

12.14 When officiating at weddings and funerals the clergy should ensure that only those fees prescribed by the Archbishops' Council in a Parochial Fees Order, reasonable travel expenses and genuine extras are requested from those with whom they make arrangements. When a marriage service or funeral service is being conducted only statutory fees and genuine extras (such as payments to organists, singers and bellringers) may be charged.

Well-being

13 **You cannot bear the weight of this calling in your own strength . . .**

13.1 The clergy minister by grace through their own broken humanity, being aware of their own need to receive ministry.

13.2 In exercising their ministry, the clergy respond to the call of our Lord Jesus Christ. The development of their discipleship is in the discipline of prayer, worship, Bible study and the discernment of the prompting of the Holy Spirit. The clergy should make sure that time and resources are available for their own personal and spiritual life and take responsibility for their own ongoing training and development.

13.3 Spiritual discernment can be facilitated by sharing the journey of faith with another person. A minister should have someone outside the work situation to whom to turn for help.

13.4 Ministers holding office under common tenure have a legal obligation to cooperate in arrangements made by the diocesan bishop for ministerial development review, and to participate in appropriate continuing ministerial education. Ministers who are not subject to common tenure should also, as a matter of good practice, ensure that arrangements are in place for their ministry to be reviewed on a regular basis and for their ongoing ministerial education.

13.5 Both formal ministerial development review and discussion with a spiritual director or companion should offer the opportunity for the clergy to reflect on whether they are giving sufficient time and attention to family life, friendship, recreation and renewal and to consider any health issues.

Care for the Carers

14 Brothers and sisters ... Will you uphold and encourage them in their ministry?

14.1 'Care for the carers' is fundamental. The clergy need to be supported and the laity have a particular and significant role in the pastoral care of the clergy.

The clergy and those who support them should be aware of the Ministry Division publication *Dignity at Work* (2008) and its recommendations concerning bullying, harassment, and accusation at work.

14.2 The bishop takes responsibility for the welfare of the clergy when receiving the oath of canonical obedience. This responsibility is shared with suffragan and area bishops, archdeacons, and rural and area deans.

14.3 Care of the clergy is a responsibility shared between the PCC and Diocesan Authorities.

Many of these responsibilities are spelled out in the *Statement of Particulars* under Common Tenure and in Diocesan Regulations. The PCC is responsible for the provision of adequate administrative assistance, reimbursement in full of ministerial expenses (see The Parochial Expenses of the Clergy, Ministry Division, 2002) available online at *www.churchofengland.org/clergy-office-holders/remuneration-and-conditions-of-service-committee/the-parochial-expenses-of-the-clergy.aspx*) and for ensuring a safe environment in the church and its surroundings in which to work.

Where the PCC is the relevant housing provider, it has responsibilities for the maintenance and upkeep of the clergy housing. The responsibilities of Bishop and Diocese are as set out in the *Statement of Particulars* and Diocesan Clergy Handbook, and in the *Green Guide* published by the Church Commissioners. The *Statement of Particulars* includes provision for holidays, an annual retreat, upkeep of the parsonage house, and entitlement to release for extra-parochial ministry.

14.4 As part of good stewardship, those who occupy either a parsonage house or housing provided by the Diocese or PCC must take proper care of the property and should be aware of the requirement to allow access for both inspections and works to take place.

14.5 Power is exercised and experienced in many ways, and the clergy should beware of the potential of using their position to bully others. Equally those who have the responsibility of caring for the clergy should be aware that bullying can be exercised both by church authorities and by parishioners.

14.6 The clergy should be encouraged to develop opportunities for mutual support and pastoral care within chapters, cell groups, or other peer-groupings. All the clergy should also be encouraged to have a spiritual director, soul friend or confessor to support their spiritual life and help to develop their growth in self-understanding. If required, help should be given in finding such a person.

14.7 In ministries where the clergy have both a sector and a parochial responsibility, there should be a clear understanding between diocese, parish and the minister concerned about where the boundaries lie.

14.8 Support and advice on the practical, psychological and emotional issues involved should be readily available to clergy approaching retirement and to their families.

14.9 The bishop and those exercising pastoral care of the clergy should both by word and example actively encourage the clergy to adopt a healthy life-style which should include adequate time for leisure, through taking days off and their full holidays, developing interests outside their main area of ministry, and maintaining a commitment to the care and development of themselves and their personal relationships. Helping the clergy understand and overcome unrealistic expectations needs to be a priority.

Did you know that SPCK is a registered charity?

As well as publishing great books by leading Christian authors, we also . . .

. . . make assemblies meaningful and fun for over a million children by running www.assemblies.org.uk, a popular website that provides free assembly scripts for teachers. For many children, school assembly is the only contact they have with Christian faith and culture, and the only time in their week for spiritual reflection.

. . . help prisoners to become confident readers with our easy-to-read stories. Poor literacy is a huge barrier to rehabilitation. Prisoners identify with the believable heroes of our gritty fiction. At the same time, questions at the end of each chapter help them to examine their choices from a moral perspective and to build their reading confidence.

. . . support student ministers overseas in their training through partnerships in the Global South.

Please support these great schemes: visit www.spck.org.uk/support-us to find out more.